Teach Yourself VISUALLY™

Poker

Teach Yourself VISUALLY™

Poker

Visual®

by Dan Ramsey

WILEY

Wiley Publishing, Inc.

Library of Congress Control Number: 2005939199

ISBN-13: 978-0-471-79906-1
ISBN-10: 0-471-79906-8

Printed in the United States of America

10 9 8 7 6 5 4 3 2 1

Book production by Wiley Publishing, Inc. Composition Services

Praise for the Teach Yourself VISUALLY Series

I just had to let you and your company know how great I think your books are. I just purchased my third Visual book (my first two are dog-eared now!) and, once again, your product has surpassed my expectations. The expertise, thought, and effort that go into each book are obvious, and I sincerely appreciate your efforts. Keep up the wonderful work!

—Tracey Moore (Memphis, TN)

I have several books from the Visual series and have always found them to be valuable resources.

—Stephen P. Miller (Ballston Spa, NY)

Thank you for the wonderful books you produce. It wasn't until I was an adult that I discovered how I learn—visually. Although a few publishers out there claim to present the material visually, nothing compares to Visual books. I love the simple layout. Everything is easy to follow. And I understand the material! You really know the way I think and learn. Thanks so much!

—Stacey Han (Avondale, AZ)

Like a lot of other people, I understand things best when I see them visually. Your books really make learning easy and life more fun.

—John T. Frey (Cadillac, MI)

I am an avid fan of your Visual books. If I need to learn anything, I just buy one of your books and learn the topic in no time. Wonders! I have even trained my friends to give me Visual books as gifts.

—Illona Bergstrom (Aventura, FL)

I write to extend my thanks and appreciation for your books. They are clear, easy to follow, and straight to the point. Keep up the good work! I bought several of your books and they are just right! No regrets! I will always buy your books because they are the best.

—Seward Kollie (Dakar, Senegal)

Credits

Acquisitions Editor
Pam Mourouzis

Project Editor
Suzanne Snyder

Copy Editor
Lori Cates Hand

Technical Editor
David Galt

Editorial Manager
Christina Stambaugh

Publisher
Cindy Kitchel

Vice President and Executive Publisher
Kathy Nebenhaus

Interior Design
Kathie Rickard
Elizabeth Brooks

Cover Design
José Almaguer

Interior Photography
Matt Bowen

Special Thanks...

To the following casinos for granting us permission to photograph.

- Robinson Rancheria Resort & Casino
- Sho-Ka-Wah Casino

About the Author

Popular author **Dan Ramsey** shares his extensive knowledge of home, casino, and online poker through hundreds of instructional photos and drawings to make learning—and winning—the world's favorite game easier. Dan has written dozens of how-to books for consumers and business. Visit Dan's Web site at www.TYVPoker.com.

Acknowledgments

Poker is a game of skill and luck. So is writing. I'm lucky to have the help of many people and businesses in developing and illustrating this book for you.

I especially want to thank Robinson Rancheria Resort & Casino (Scott Sirois, Christina Roth, and crew) in Nice, California, and Sho-Ka-Wah Casino (John Straus, Tracy Anderson, and Bob Krofchik) in Hopland, California, for allowing me to take photos in their facilities.

Thanks also go to Kal Suurkast and Anita Ayre of Bodog Poker; Jane Hastings of FatCat Poker; Chuck Humphrey of gambling-law-us.com; Dan Paymar of Optimum Video Poker Software; Richard Harris, John Shepherd and Rupam Deb of PartyPoker; Robert Yee of PokerInspector; Alan Hays of SmartDraw; and Bob Wilson and Mike Frederick of Wilson Software. Additional thanks go to rec.gambling.poker, ConJelCo/StatKing, UltimateBet, U.S. Playing Card Co., and WizardOfOdds.com for research assistance.

Editorially, I am very lucky. The guidance of Pam Mourouzis, Suzanne Snyder, Lori Cates Hand, and Christina Stambaugh at Wiley Publishing, Inc., has made this a better book than I initially wrote. A special "thank you" goes to technical editor David Galt for his thorough review. Thanks to my publisher and friend Cindy Kitchel for getting this project moving in the first place. And thanks to Neil Soderstrom for his diligence.

Family members served as models for this book, including Heather, Aaron, and Ashley Luedemann and my wife, Judy. Thank you all!

I am very lucky to gain a poker education from my son, Brendon Ramsey. He contributed much to this book as well as serving as my primary photo model. I dedicate this book to him.

Table of Contents

chapter 5 **Omaha Poker**

chapter 6 **Play Home Poker**

chapter 7 — Play Online Poker

chapter 8 — Play Video Poker

chapter 9 — Play Casino Poker

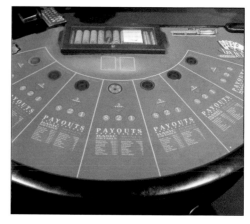

chapter 10 — Play Tournament Poker

chapter 1

The Game of Poker

Poker is a game of luck, skill, and money played with cards. The more skill a player develops, the better the "luck" and the higher the winnings. Even if poker is played for matchsticks, winning is fun. This first chapter introduces you to the basic rules and terminology of all poker games, whether played at home, in a casino or card club, with a hand-held game machine, or online. Once you understand the game of poker, you can increase your odds of winning—and increase your fun!

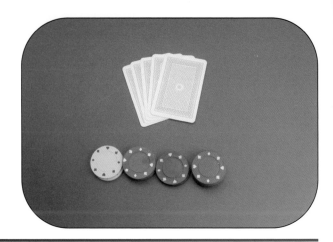

Poker is a game—an activity engaged in for diversion or amusement. Like all games, the goal is to win. Unlike many other games, you keep score using money or its equivalent (chips). Players win money from other players by holding the best-ranking hand or by pretending to (which is called *bluffing*), and forcing other players to relinquish their right to the money everyone has bet, which is called the *pot*.

A *hand* is the cards dealt to a player. The *ranking* of a hand simply means the probability of being dealt the cards randomly from the deck. "Poker Ranks," later in this chapter, explains ranking further.

Most versions of poker end with active players comparing the best five cards they have. In many versions, each player is dealt only five; however, in games such as Texas Hold'em and Omaha, players are dealt more cards, although they can use only five of them.

"The Game of Poker" flowchart on the facing page summarizes how most poker games are played. Follow it from Start to End and read its explanatory notes for an overview of the structure of poker.

Alhough there are hundreds of poker games, they fit into just a couple of types with many variations. If the cards are dealt face down so that other players cannot see them, the game is from the *draw* family (see Chapter 2). If some of the cards are dealt face up, the game is from the *stud* family (see Chapter 3). Two variations of stud poker have become very popular and have earned their own chapters: Texas Hold'em (Chapter 4) and Omaha (Chapter 5).

Where you play poker also dictates how you play it. A friendly poker game at home is played with very different strategies than a "free" online game or a "real money" no-limit casino game. Chapters 6 through 11 present popular games and winning strategies for each venue.

The bottom line to poker is this: The greater your knowledge and skill, the more you can profit from luck.

The Game of Poker

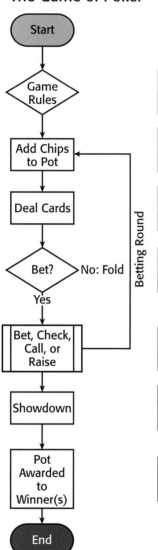

Start

Game Rules

The game, banker, dealer(s), deck, ante, bets, raises, and limits are agreed upon.

Add Chips to Pot

To encourage betting on hands, an initial bet (ante or blind) is put in the pot at the table center.

Deal Cards

Cards are dealt one at a time clockwise around the table to all active players.

Bet? No: Fold

A player who folds gives up all rights to winning the pot during this hand.

Yes

Bet, Check, Call, or Raise

Each player in turn places a bet, bets zero (checks), matches (calls), or increases (raises) the bet. Once everyone has an equal amount in the pot, or folds, the next cards are dealt and the next betting round begins.

Betting Round

Showdown

Once all cards required by the game are dealt and all players are equally invested in the pot or fold, the winner, based on game rules, is announced and the pot distributed.

Pot Awarded to Winner(s)

Any or all players may leave the game and, if available, others may join for the next hand(s).

End

History

Poker is based on an ancient game that traces its origins back to Persia, through Russia, France, and other countries. The game played today as "poker" is very American, loosely developed from a French game called "poqué" meaning "tired."

The Origins of Today's Poker

Game experts agree that poker as played today originated with the riverboat gamblers who plied the Mississippi River from New Orleans north. The earliest games dealt each player five cards on which the players, in turn, bet and raised. No additional cards were dealt.

Now played worldwide (and even online, as shown in this figure), poker retains American geographical names such as "Texas Hold'em," "Omaha," "Cincinnati," and "Chicago"—even when played in Berlin, Bangkok, and Baghdad.

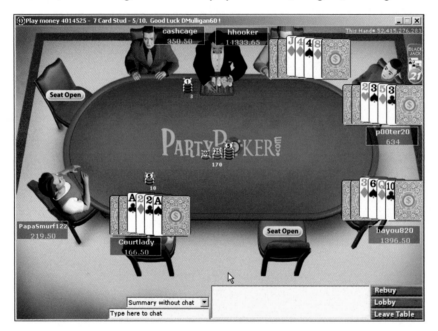

Poker's Popularity

There are now hundreds of games that follow the basic rules of poker, with numerous variations to make it more interesting to players of all types and interests. Over the past 30 years, Texas Hold'em has become the most popular of all poker games worldwide, primarily due to its selection as the deciding game for the World Series of Poker (WSoP), the ultimate showdown for poker players.

Poker continues to grow and evolve, with versions played differently at home, in casinos, at card clubs, online, and in other locations. Even casinos have variations or favorite games depending on local tastes. Video poker (see Chapter 8) is increasingly popular at casinos, though it isn't the same game as played at casino card tables.

Cards

Poker cards are approximately 2½ inches wide by 3½ inches tall. The backs in a deck of cards have a common design and color, whereas the fronts (or *faces*) are individual. A standard deck of poker playing cards includes 52 cards. Many decks also include two additional cards, called *Jokers*, which are used in some poker games. In addition, some decks include a printed instruction card or a list of hand rankings for reference.

Suits and Ranks (Cards)

Poker and other playing cards have four *suits* or emblems:

- clubs (♣)
- diamonds (♦)
- hearts (♥)
- spades (♠)

Each suit consists of 13 ranks of cards. The ranks in the suit are as follows:

- A = Ace
- K = King
- Q = Queen
- J = Jack
- T = Ten
- 9 = Nine
- 8 = Eight

- 7 = Seven
- 6 = Six
- 5 = Five
- 4 = Four
- 3 = Three (or trey)
- 2 = Deuce

Multiply four suits by 13 ranks and you get 52 playing cards in a poker deck.

Shuffling

To make sure that the cards are randomly distributed to players, the deck is shuffled between games. Here's how to shuffle:

1 Separate the deck of playing cards into two approximately even stacks.

2 Hold one stack in each hand with your thumb under the stack and the next three fingers on top of the stack.

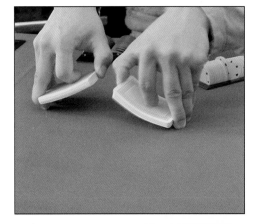

3 Move the stacks so that your thumbs are nearly touching.

4 Move your thumbs away from the center so that the individual card edges are released and randomly fall to the table into one new stack.

5 Push the shuffled cards together into a uniform stack.

Chips

Poker is played for money; but players do not always use cash. Home games often use coins (pennies, nickels, dimes, and quarters); casino and card room poker games, however, use poker chips to represent money. In games where speed and accuracy are important, color-coded chips make counting and betting more efficient—and easier to verify.

Types of Chips

HOME-GAME CHIPS

Poker-chip sets for home games can be purchased inexpensively, many with the suggested value printed on them to avoid confusion.

Players in home games may also choose to use coins, matchsticks, or another object to keep track of betting as long as all players agree on the value of the tokens.

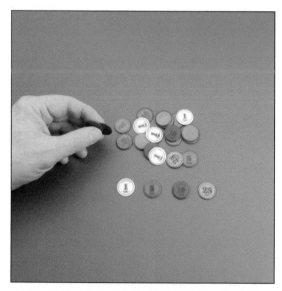

CASINO CHIPS

Poker tournaments, casinos, and card rooms use four or more colors of playing chips. Casinos and card rooms may use their own system for color-coding chips, although most venues within a gaming location may standardize colors and values. Commonly used colors include white, red, blue, yellow, green, black, and gold. For example, many casinos use the following relative values:

White = 1
Red = 5
Blue = 10
Green = 25
Black = 100
Purple = 500

ONLINE CHIPS

Online poker games may use a color-coded system as well as mark chips with their values. In the online game shown in this figure, the colors and values are clearly indicated.

TIP

When exchanging cash for chips with the banker, make sure you understand the value of each chip. If in doubt, ask the banker or dealer.

The cards a player holds are called a *hand*. There are nine ranks of hands in the game of poker. The player holding—or bluffing—the best hand at the end of the game wins.

In most poker games, it is the hand with the highest rank that wins the pot. In some games it is agreed that the lowest-ranking hand wins. Some games with a large number of players agree to split the pot equally between the highest and lowest hands, called *high-low* (hi-lo) or *split* games, as shown here.

Highest Ranking Hands, in Order

Following are the highest to lowest ranks among poker hands. Among hands, higher ranks beat lower ranks. For example, a king-high flush beats a queen-high flush and a pair of tens beat a pair of sixes.

STRAIGHT FLUSH

A *straight flush* consists of five cards of the same suit, in sequence. If the sequence is ace, king, queen, jack, and 10 of the same suit, as shown in this photo, it is called a Royal Flush.

FOUR-OF-A-KIND

Four-of-a-kind (quad) is made up of four cards of the same rank, plus a fifth unrelated or odd card. Shown here is a four-of-a-kind hand comprised of four aces and a king.

FULL HOUSE

A *full house* consists of three-of-a-kind plus a pair of another kind or rank. Shown here is a full house composed of three aces and a pair of kings, known as "aces full of kings."

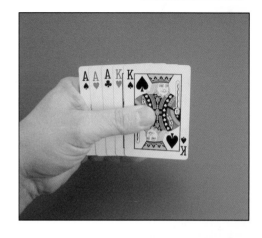

FLUSH

A *flush* is made up of five cards of the same suit, but not in sequence. Shown here is a heart flush.

STRAIGHT

A *straight* consists of five cards in sequence, but not of the same suit. Shown here is a queen-high straight.

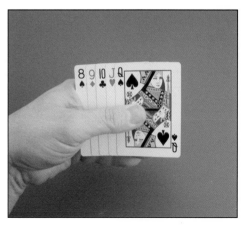

CONTINUED ON NEXT PAGE

THREE-OF-A-KIND

Three-of-a-kind consists of three cards ("trips" or a "set") of the same rank, with two odd cards. Pictured are three 9s, an ace, and a jack.

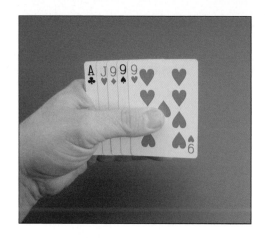

TWO PAIR

A *two-pair* hand is made up of two sets of cards of matching rank, with a fifth unrelated card. Here are two pair: queens and 9s.

ONE PAIR

A *one-pair* hand consists of two cards of matching rank, with three unrelated cards. Shown in the photo are a pair of aces, a 10♣, a 9♥, and a 5♥.

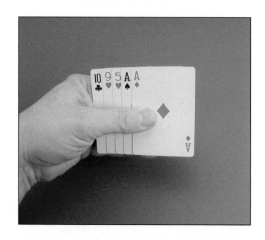

HIGH CARD

The value of a high-card hand is determined by the rank of the highest card, depending on the rules of the game. In this case, it would be the ace in an ace-high hand, sometimes called "no pair."

LOWEST HAND

Following is the lowest rank among poker hands, an ace-low straight flush. Other low rankings depend on the specific game rules.

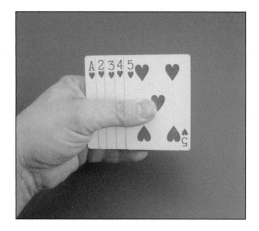

TIP

Many poker players prefer playing games that follow high-low or low hand rankings. The most popular high-low games are Stud/8 (see Chapter 3) and Omaha/8 (see Chapter 5). The most popular low-only game is Razz, a form of Seven-Card Stud (see Chapter 3)

Odds

Poker is a game of probabilities, or the odds of something occurring or not occurring. For example, if you are dealt three cards, the odds are about 5 to 1 that two of the cards will be of the same rank, a pair. Because poker is a game of chance, the more you know the odds of something occurring, the better your betting decisions will be and the more you will win.

CARD ODDS

The number of different five-card poker hands possible in a deck of 52 cards is 2,598,960. The odds of being dealt a royal flush (ace-high straight flush) are 1 in 649,740 hands, and many players never get one. (If you played 60 hands an hour for 40 hours a week, odds are that you would be dealt a royal flush every 5.2 years.)

Possible Poker Hands (52-Card Deck)	
Ranking Order	*Chance of Being Dealt in Original Five Cards*
Royal Flush	1 in 649,740
Straight Flush	1 in 72,193
Four-of-a-kind	1 in 4,165
Full house	1 in 694
Flush	1 in 509
Straight	1 in 255
Three-of-a-kind	1 in 47
Two pair	1 in 21
One pair	1 in 2.4
No-pair hand	1 in 2

Each type of poker game has supplementary odds depending on how many cards are dealt to players (five, seven, or nine) and how many active players are in the game (2 to 12). Odds charts are also available to determine the chance of getting a better hand when a specific number of cards are discarded, such as in draw poker.

POT ODDS

Sometimes it's worth making an extra bet into the pot even though the odds of winning it are not high. If the chances of winning the pot are 10 to 1 and your $5 bet might win a $100 pot, the pot odds are good and may be worth the extra investment.

PEOPLE ODDS

With experience, you'll become skilled at reading other poker players, predicting what types of hands they have by the way they play (see the section "People"). You'll also be able to accurately tell whether they are bluffing. These are called *edge odds.* The laws of probability work in regard to players as well as cards and pots.

STRATEGY CARDS

Appendix A has some charts of probability. In addition, you can purchase pocket-sized odds and strategy cards at gaming bookstores, the game section of new bookstores, casinos, and online. Most casinos and many card clubs allow players to keep strategy cards in plain view when playing, especially at games aimed at beginners. Professional gamblers have them memorized.

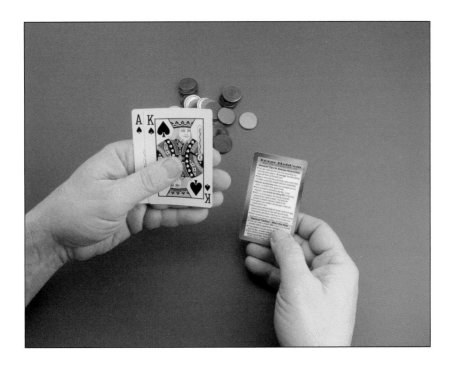

Rules

"The Game of Poker" flowchart (see page 5) shows that the first decision in poker is agreeing on the rules. At casinos, game rules are typically posted at the table, although they are written in the cryptic shorthand of poker (see Chapter 5 for more on poker shorthand).

Some poker games change at a table as selected by the dealer, a practice that is called *dealer's choice*. If you are not clear on the rules of a new game or variation, ask the dealer. Every poker player is a beginner at some time.

Limits

Many poker games have limits on the size of bets that can be made; a few are announced as *no-limit* games. Some limit is preferred, however, so that the player with the most money doesn't force others out of the game.

In a *fixed-limit* game, no player may bet or raise by more than a stipulated number of chips. In most fixed-limit games, the limit changes during the game, such as one limit before the draw or for the first two betting intervals and a higher limit afterwards, such as a $5/$10 Hold'em game that limits bets to $5 for the first two betting intervals and $10 thereafter.

A *pot-limit* game limits any bet or raise to the number of chips in the pot. If the pot and any bets before yours add up to 32 chips, the raise is limited to an additional 32 chips.

Table-stake games limit players to betting only the chips they have in front of them. They can't buy more from the banker. No-limit games are actually table-stake games as no additional chips can be purchased during the game.

In some games, a player puts all of his or her chips in the pot. This is called *all-in.* Betting continues with other players contributing to a second or side pot. Winners may be awarded one or both of the pots depending on the showdown, when all betting is over and players show their cards to determine the winner(s).

TIP

A poker showdown is educational. Players can determine whether other players hold a good hand or are bluffing. Smart players may show their cards, even if they know they won't win, in order to make other players know they were bluffing.

Banker

One of the first steps in setting up a poker game is establishing the *banker.* Casinos and card clubs have their own bankers. Home games require that a banker be selected.

The banker in a poker game is someone who sells and redeems chips for players. In home games, the banker may be a player; or, if coins are used instead of chips, no banker is needed. In card-room games, the banker often is also the dealer. In casinos, the banker may be a dealer, or there may be a separate person at the table or a nearby window where chips are sold and bought.

Bankers do not charge a fee or a premium for the service. However, casinos may require a fee for some types of transactions, such as out-of-area checks or credit-card transactions.

Dealer

The *dealer* in a poker game distributes the cards to players according to the rules of the game. The dealer shuffles the cards and then deals them one at a time from the top of the deck, clockwise to each active player. The dealer also manages the pot, announcing who is to bet and, in some games, the rank of cards shown.

In some games, the dealer is also a player, and the role of dealer rotates around the table. If the dealer is a player, he or she acts last in the betting rounds. In some games, the dealer also chooses the game and announces the rules.

Betting

Poker is about betting whether the player's cards are of a higher (or lower) rank than other players' cards. The decisions of when and how much to bet are learned skills that minimize luck and maximize winning.

Betting Lingo

POT

The purpose of poker is to win money in the pot. The *pot* is the aggregate of chips or money at stake in the current deal. The pot also is known as the *pool* or the *kitty.* During a round of betting, once all players have contributed equally to the pot or have *folded* (relinquished any rights to the pot), the pot is said to be *right* (or *balanced*), and the next round of cards is dealt or the hands are compared in the *showdown.* (Refer to "The Game of Poker" flowchart on page 5.) Note that the pot in most home or friendly games is a loose pile of chips in the center of the table added to by each player; however, dealers at casinos and card rooms stack and manage the pot chips.

ANTE

To encourage players to bet toward winning the pot, an ante or blind is contributed to the pot before cards are dealt. An *ante* is a contribution made by each player. A *blind* is a contribution made by a few selected players, typically the two to the left of the dealer. In Hold'em, for example, the game may begin with the first player to the left being required to make a *small blind* contribution of half the initial betting limit—$1 in the case of a $2 limit. The player to the left of the small blind makes a *big blind* contribution—$2 in the case of a $2 limit.

BET

To *bet* is to offer a wager on the outcome of an event. If the player determines that the cards dealt are of sufficient rank to have potential value against other players' cards, the player bets a specific amount of money. The player makes a bet because he or she believes that the cards held are, or have reasonable odds to become, the best hand at the table.

FOLD

To *fold* is to withdraw from the current deal and relinquish all rights to the pot. If the player determines that the cards dealt are not of sufficient rank to have potential value against other players' cards, the player folds. Players signify folding by turning their cards face down in front of them. They also may announce "I fold."

CALL

To *call* is to make a bet that is exactly equal to the preceding active player's bet. The player announces "I call," or "I see."

CHECK

To *check* is to make a bet of zero, retaining rights to the pot without adding to it. The player announces "I check." The first player in a round may check; then subsequent players may check. However, if a subsequent player makes a bet, the bet must be called or cards folded to ensure that all active players are equally invested in the pot.

RAISE

To *raise* a bet is to increase it over the required amount. If the bet is $10, subsequent players may call (match), raise (increase) it, or fold. If the bet is raised, all players get the opportunity to call the raise or fold. A player makes a raise because he or she is relatively certain that the cards he or she holds are the best hand at the table. The player announces "I raise" or, for subsequent raises, "I reraise."

Poker is a game of analyzing the relative value of cards you hold versus the value of the cards other players hold. Because you cannot see their cards, you must learn how to "read" the players. Alhough this skill comes with experience, there are proven techniques for analyzing people and cards through what are called *tells*.

A tell is an outward indicator of internal thought. Many players attempt to minimize facial expressions and other actions with a "poker face" so other players can't read what they are thinking and—thus—analyze their cards. Some players wear sunglasses, even when in a low-lit casino, to keep others from reading their eyes

Reading Tells

KNOW YOURSELF

Other players at the poker table will be similar to you in many ways. Knowing what you would do with a specific hand will help you analyze the tells of other players. With a pair of aces, you might cover your mouth to hide a grin. With a straight, you might act anxious for the next round of betting. With a full house, you might grab your chest.

BLUFFING

A *bluff* is when a player makes a bet on a hand that he or she does not believe is the best hand at the table. By acting as if they hold the best hand—by raising on a weaker hand such as pair of nines—the player may encourage other players to misread the hand and to fold.

Player Types

You will soon recognize that players can be grouped by types who often identify themselves by facial expressions, dress, or mannerisms. Knowing the common types will help you read other players and learn how to respond to their playing methods—and win more often.

- **Loose players:** *Loose players* play all but the worst hands. They more frequently attempt to bluff, especially late in the hand, if they realize that they don't have the best hand at the table. Loose players are invested in most pots, but win few. Loose players are impatient. They often are referred to as *fish* because there are so many of them.

- **Tight players:** *Tight players* play only the best hands. They rarely bluff because they strongly believe that their hand is the best one at the table. Tight players invest in fewer pots and win more of them. Tight players are patient. They don't play or bet weak hands.

- **Aggressive players:** *Aggressive players* prefer to raise or to fold. They know that they will win some hands with poor cards due to their aggressiveness by causing others to fold.

- **Passive players:** *Passive players* prefer to call or to fold and rarely raise. They know that they will win some hands, but prefer not to lose on others.

- **Most players:** Most poker players are a combination of these types, with one or two characteristics more dominant than others. In addition, some players purposely display one type of action periodically just to confuse players who are trying to read them.

Etiquette

Poker is like any other human interaction in that there are rules for conduct that should be followed. Breaking these rules can earn you the label of "bad sport" and eliminate you from future play. Fortunately, most of these poker etiquette rules are common sense and easy to learn.

Etiquette Rules to Follow

PLAY IN TURN

Poker play typically begins with the person on the left side of the dealer and continues clockwise. In some games, however, the first player to bet is the one with the highest or lowest card showing; then the clockwise rule begins. Never play out of turn, even if you've decided to raise or fold. Wait until it is your turn to do so because it might impact the decisions of those before or after you.

To assist in identifying the dealer, some card games and venues use a chip-like marker with "D" or "Dealer" on it that is placed to the left of the active dealer, as in this photo. It's called the "dealer chip" or "dealer button."

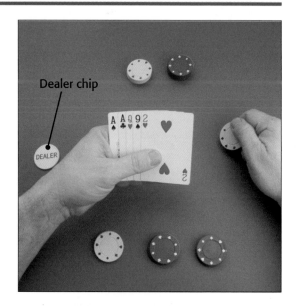

Dealer chip

NEVER LOOK AT OTHER PEOPLE'S HANDS

Cards dealt face down are intended for only the owner's eyes. Do not attempt to look at these private—or *hole*—cards. In fact, avoid looking at or near a player who is viewing his or her hole cards. Many poker games have some cards face up that can—and should—be viewed toward analyzing the players' hands. If a dealer accidentally flips up a hole card when dealing, the hand may be called *dead* and must be redealt.

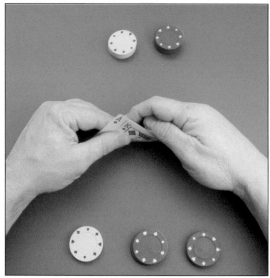

Here are some other etiquette rules to follow when playing poker:

- **Don't Discuss Active Hands:** The dealer might routinely identify the hands or potential hands ("possible straight" or "pair of queens"), but players typically don't comment on hands. However, a few will "trash-talk" as a distraction to upset other players and make them *tilt,* or play emotionally.

- **Muck Your Cards:** If you fold your cards, place them in the discard or "muck" pile face down near the center of the table where the dealer can reach them. These cards are then disqualified from further play and cannot be viewed during the current game. If any one player sees another's mucked hand, all players have the right to see it.

- **Be a Good Winner:** Congratulations! You've won the pot! Don't dance, jump up and down, or make rude remarks to any other player or the dealer. Once it is acknowledged that you won the pot, simply move it in front of you and stack your chips. If someone compliments the hand, thank them.

- **Be a Courteous Loser:** Someone had a higher flush or full house than yours. You lost—maybe big. Don't scowl, curse, or make angry gestures at other players or the dealer. Accept your losses, learn from them, and put your ante in for the next hand. It might be a winner.

- **Know Your Game's Etiquette:** Each poker game has a few etiquette rules of its own. Also, poker venues have different rules for behaving when playing. Some are covered in future chapters. Others you will discover by watching others play, win, and lose. Enjoy!

TIP

The best advice from pros is: *Know why you are playing poker.* If you prefer friendly, home games with little or no money, stick to that goal and don't try to play cutthroat poker. However, if your goal is to play poker as an income source, play low-stake games until you develop your poker skills before moving to the big-money tables.

Poker is a game of making good decisions based on knowledge and experience. Knowing the basics of the game, how it is played, and how to interpret your own cards is important to all variations of the game of poker, as is knowing how to read the "tells" of other players, and having a knowledge of odds. Learning the rules of specific games is vital to success, too.

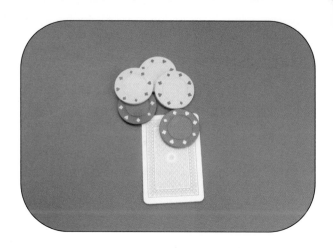

Where to Gain Experience

Experience comes from actually playing the game. Most new players learn techniques playing with friends at home, watching games on TV, or playing online. These are inexpensive sources of experience. This book will save you hundreds of hours of learning by playing, but you still must play poker.

Later chapters offer tips and strategies for playing poker at home, online, in casinos and card rooms, and in tournaments. To gain winning experience for these venues, I recommend that you find a source for free or low-cost poker games and make as many mistakes as possible, learning from each one. Toward that end, here are proven methods for building poker smarts.

FAMILY POKER

Ask around among family and friends and you might find a few who are willing to teach you what they know about poker without taking your money. Play for pennies, buttons, matchsticks, or whatever form of low-cost exchange you can find. Remember to supplement your practice with formal instruction (this book) or other resources so that you don't pick up bad habits.

SOFTWARE POKER

There are numerous free and low-cost poker programs available for your computer. One is Fat Cat Poker, which pits you against four other players and the dealer in games such as Five-Card Stud, Seven-Card Stud, High Chicago, Hold'em, and two versions of Five-Card Draw. It also offers game statistics for the "live" games. The software is inexpensive and a free demo version is available online at www.accidental.com.

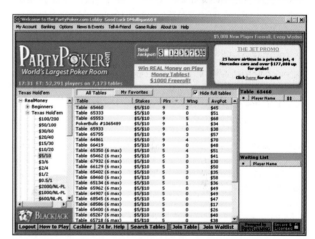

ONLINE POKER

There are dozens of popular poker sites on the Internet where you can play free games with players of all skill levels. Chapter 7 offers more specifics and some winning strategies. Meanwhile, if you have Internet access, visit www.pokerroom.com or www.ultimatebet.com for the software and requirements to set up a free account. You'll soon be playing fun poker with people around the world. It's great experience for building your poker smarts.

GAME PLAYERS

Many of the portable game players, such as Game Boy, and even many cellular telephones, have basic poker games you can play anywhere. It's not how the game is played at Atlantic City or a Gardena card club, but it's still fun. You'll memorize the poker ranks and discover your own strategies for playing the world's favorite game.

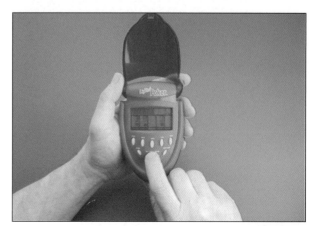

Poker is not illegal. You can play it anywhere with anyone without worrying about the "poker police" taking you off to jail. However, betting is *not* legal everywhere. In many places, you cannot legally flip a coin and bet money on the outcome. Nor can you play poker for money. This section takes a closer look at the laws.

Gambling vs. Gaming

Gambling is the illegal betting on an outcome, whether it is a horse race or a Royal Flush. Gaming, on the other hand, is betting or placing a bet where it is legal. Gaming is legal when authorized by the state, such as in a lottery, or when done at a location licensed by the state, such as a Las Vegas casino, or by the federal government, as at an Indian casino (shown).

Is playing poker for money online legal? It is if the state in which you live or play allows it. Currently, few jurisdictions allow online betting, so it is considered gambling. However, laws are being worked on to regulate and tax online gambling. At that time, it will be considered online gaming. Until then, players depend on the fact that laws against online gambling are not widely enforced.

Gaming laws are based on whether the game is won by skill or by chance, whether it is considered a social or a professional game, and whether the infraction and penalties are petty crimes, misdemeanors, or felonies.

For additional information on laws governing poker and other games of chance, visit www.gambling-law-us.com.

Taxing Your Poker Winnings

Whether your poker winnings are subject to taxation is a different matter. They are. Whether the winning came from gaming (legal betting) or gambling (illegal betting), you are required by law to pay taxes on the proceeds (winnings less losses and expenses). In fact, gaming casinos, card rooms, and other venues are required to report larger winnings to the state and federal government. If you win the big jackpot in the World Series of Poker, not only will all your relatives see it on television, the Internal Revenue Service and others with taxation jurisdiction will know. In some cases, an estimated tax of approximately 25 percent will be held back from your winnings until you file your income taxes. The minimum at which winnings are reported depends on the size of the prize, the state and federal authorities, and other regulations. Frequently, a single win of $1,200 or more requires automatic reporting.

Good advice is to keep track of all poker winnings and losses (with a system such as Stat King, shown), including travel and related expenses. A tax advisor can help you determine what is and isn't deductible.

Good luck!

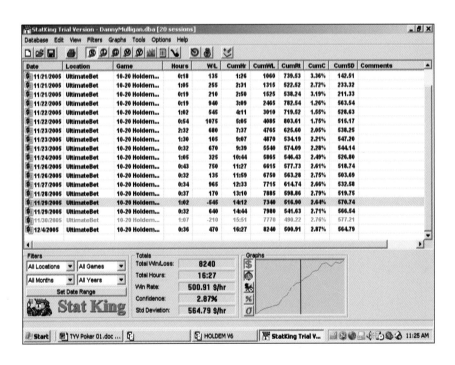

2

Draw Poker

Draw poker is the easiest type of poker game to learn and to play. It is also one of the oldest poker game types. Commonly seen played in Western movies, draw poker is fun and challenging for adults and younger players. Five cards are dealt face down to each player, followed by an interval of betting. Once the pot is "right," each player may request some replacement cards; and then the final betting interval occurs. Remaining players show their cards to determine the winner of the pot. It's that easy. Of course, there are many winning strategies to discover, as well as many variations to this popular poker game. This chapter is a great place to start enjoying poker.

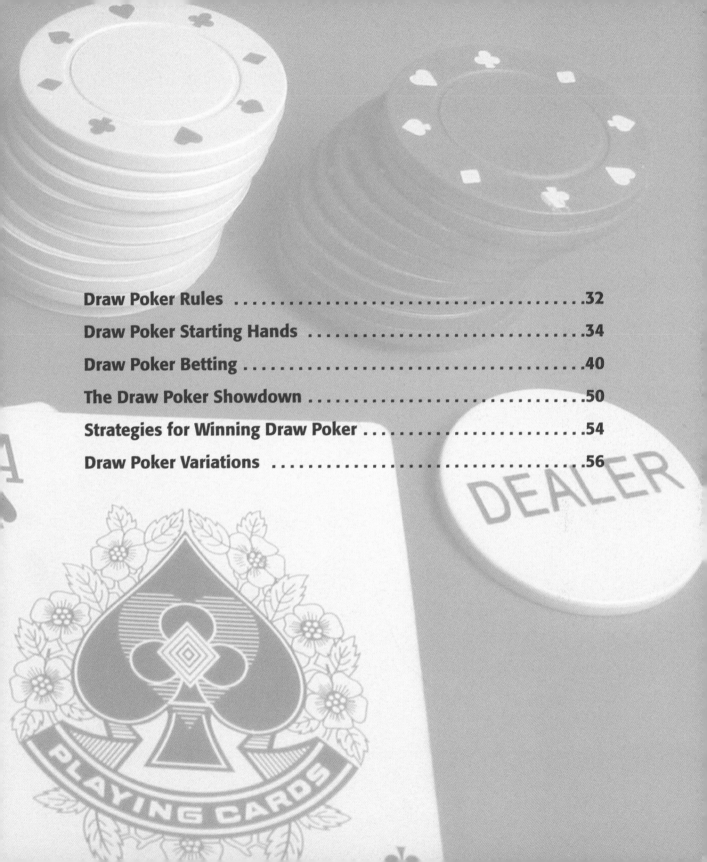

Draw Poker Rules

Although it was one of the earliest poker game types, draw poker is not played extensively in modern gaming venues such as casinos and card clubs. It is, however, the most popular home game because of its simplicity. It's fun to play.

The Game

Draw poker is played with a standard 52-card pack of playing cards. As with other poker games, the object is to win the pot by holding at showdown a hand of cards of higher rank than any other player or by being the only remaining player. The standard ranks of poker hands are as presented in Chapter 1. Low and High-Low Draw poker variations also are played. These are covered later in this chapter in the section "Draw Poker Variations."

Two to ten players may simultaneously play draw poker; however, six is the common limit without having to shuffle and redeal the discards.

Once the game rules are agreed upon, all players make the initial bet (the ante) into the common pot.

Five cards are then dealt one at a time clockwise around the table to all active players.

Many draw-poker games, by mutual agreement, require that the player who first bets must hold *openers,* or cards of at least a specified rank, such as a pair of jacks or better. Once one player meets the requirement and bets or *opens,* all other players may call or raise the bet. If no player can open, all cards are discarded and redealt, with the pot remaining for the next hand and a new ante.

Betting

Beginning with the player to the left of the dealer, each player places a bet, checks, calls, raises, or folds based on an analysis of the starting hand.

The first betting round is complete when all players either have matched the investment of all other active players or have folded, relinquishing rights to win the pot. Except in no-limit draw poker, the players must conform to the game's minimum and maximum bet limits.

The dealer then asks each active player, beginning on the left and working clockwise, if they want to discard and draw new cards. "How many?"

Note: *Standard draw poker allows up to three replacement cards, although players can agree before the game on four or even five draw cards.*

The players respond to the dealer by indicating how many cards they want to draw and placing an equal number of cards in front of them as discards. The dealer then deals an equal number of cards, one at a time, to the player. A player who does not want to replace cards *stands pat.*

Once all players have drawn, a second betting interval begins with the next active player to the dealer's left. Each player in turn may bet, check, call, raise, or fold.

Note: *In some games there is a limit to the number of raises that players can make in a betting interval, which is commonly three.*

When the second betting interval is complete, all active players must show their cards to the dealer and other players for determination of who has the best hand(s). This is the *showdown.* The pot is distributed to the winner(s) and a new game may begin.

Draw Poker Starting Hands

As you can see, the five cards initially dealt in draw poker are very important to winning. As important are your decisions of what to discard toward holding a better hand.

Considering the Odds

Draw Poker Chances	
Hand	*Once in Approximately . . .*
Any pair or better	2 deals
Pair of jacks or better	5 deals
Pair of queens or better	6 deals
Pair of kings or better	7 deals
Pair of aces or better	9 deals
Two pairs or better	13 deals
Three-of-a-kind or better	35 deals
Straight or better	132 deals
Flush or better	273 deals
Full house or better	590 deals
Four-of-a-kind or better	3,914 deals
Straight flush or better	64,974 deals
Royal Flush	649,740 deals

Your decision on what to keep and what to discard depends on many factors, including how many cards were drawn by other players. It might seem beneficial to allow four or even five discard cards in establishing game rules; remember, however, that your opponents have the same chance as you do of improving their hands, no matter how many discard or draw cards are allowed. Three is the most commonly accepted discard/draw maximum.

If you have one pair and discard three, the odds for any improvement in your hand are about 2½-to-1, or 40 percent. The odds of discarding three and getting a second pair are 5-to-1, or 20 percent. The odds of discarding three and getting a match to your pair (for three-of-a-kind) are 8-to-1, or about 12 percent.

Making the Decision

After you consider the odds of improving a hand, making the decision of what to discard becomes easier. Holding two aces, as shown, is an easy decision. Use the "Draw Poker Chances" table (previous page) to help determine what starting hand to hold.

However, there is the *kicker*. A kicker is an extra card kept with a pair for a two-card draw. For example, let's say your initial hand is J♦-J♠-5♠-9♣-A♠. Odds tell you to keep the two jacks and discard the other three cards. Even so, many players also keep the ace as a kicker, hoping to draw another ace for two pair. At 3-to-1 odds, this is not the best bet. Chances are higher of improving the pair with three new draws rather than two (2½-to-1). Players who keep kickers are defying the odds, sometimes to make other players believe they hold three-of-a-kind (also known as trips).

The decisions in draw poker are few and relatively easy, which is why it is a popular game for beginners and for home games. To make the game more interesting, there are many variations, covered in the section "Draw Poker Variations."

CONTINUED ON NEXT PAGE

Example Game: Starting Hands

Note: *Example games in this chapter are intended for basic instruction and do not reflect poker strategies.*

PLAYER 1

No pairs, no connected cards, no more than two of any suit: this is a very weak hand.

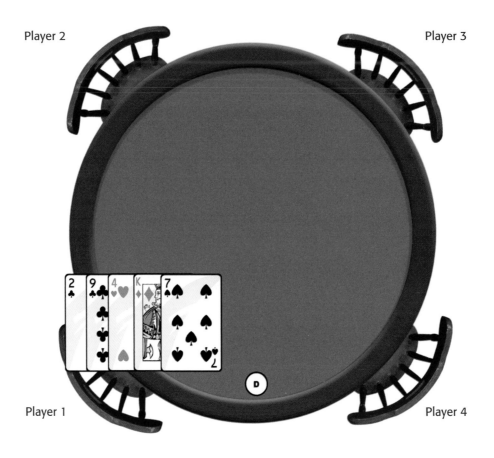

Player 2

Player 3

Player 1

Player 4

PLAYER 2

A pair of jacks and three cards of a straight (9-J-Q): the pair is the better starting (initial) hand. There are no more than two cards of any suit.

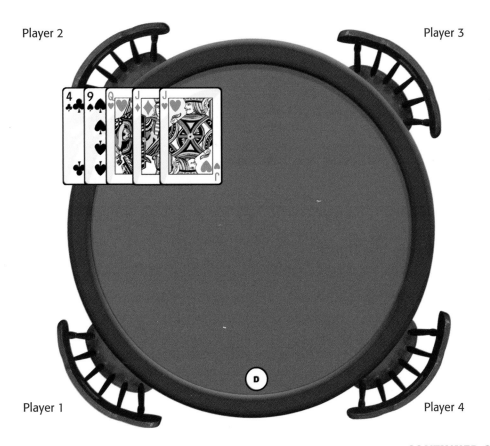

Player 2

Player 3

Player 1

Player 4

CONTINUED ON NEXT PAGE

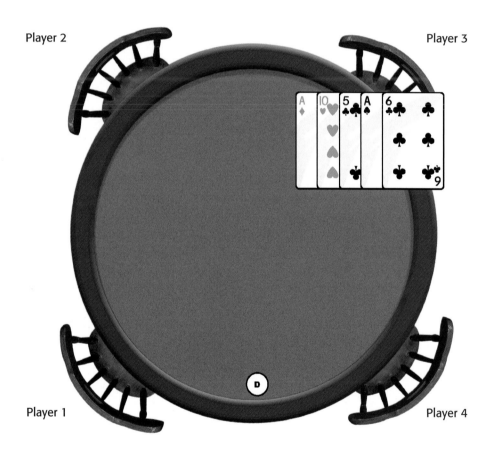

PLAYER 3

Between a pair of aces and two clubs the pair is the better starting hand.

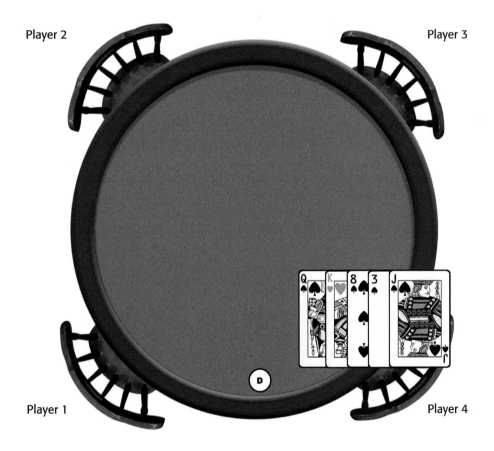

PLAYER 4

Between a flush draw (four cards of the same suit, spades) and three cards of a straight (J-Q-K) the flush draw is the better starting hand.

Player 2

Player 3

Player 1

Player 4

Draw Poker Betting

Betting is an integral part of playing any poker game, and draw poker is no exception. In fact, standard draw poker offers only two betting intervals, so understanding how and how much to bet is vital to winning pots.

A *betting interval* is the period in which bets are made. Betting may require only one time around the table, called a *betting round*, to make the pot "right," or equal. However, if a player bets rather than checking or raising a bet, a new betting round begins, ending when all active players have an equal investment in the pot.

First Interval

After the first five cards are dealt to all active players, the first interval of betting begins. Players bet on whether the hand they hold is the best or can be improved (with the draw) to be the best hand at the end of the game. Because the cards are dealt at random, there is no definitive way of knowing whether your hand is better than anyone else's—except reading your starting hand (above) and reading *tells* or behaviors (see Chapter 1). For example, in the hand shown in the photo, the player should hold the two aces and discard/draw three cards.

One of the most telling behaviors is how other players before you bet on their starting hands. Of course, this is more difficult if you are one of the first to bet, so players in the early betting positions typically bet conservatively until they know how many cards the other players draw. There might be an opportunity to increase the bet on the next round in the interval.

Remember, however, that some players purposely draw fewer cards to make other players believe they hold a better starting hand than they do. They're bluffing.

Second Interval

After all players have completed the first interval of betting and have drawn cards to replace discards (see illustration), the second and final betting interval begins. Players are betting on whether the hand they hold will be the best hand at showdown. Alternatively, they might be betting to force all other players out of the game so that they don't have to show their weak hand.

Besides the odds charts, tells can assist in deciding whether investing further in the pot might be profitable. Watch how other players respond to looking at their cards for the first time, how they handle their chips, how they bet, and any other telling responses to playing.

Many players use the *check-raise* to deceive other players into thinking that their hand is weak when it actually is strong. If no bets have been made in the round, the player *checks* (bets zero). Then if another player bets, indicating a potentially good hand, the initial player calls or even raises to suggest a possibly strong hand.

Additional winning strategies for draw poker are covered later in this chapter.

FAQ

What is the difference between a betting interval and a betting round?
An interval is the entire betting period that includes one or more rounds (around the table) before the next event (deal, showdown, and so on).

CONTINUED ON NEXT PAGE

Example Game: First Betting Interval

PLAYER 1

Though holding a weak hand, player 1 hopes to pick a better hand up on the draw. Player 1 decides to keep the highest ranking card, the king, and discard four cards, but first must place a bet on the cards held. In some draw games, the draw limit is three cards. Player 1 bets.

Player 2

Player 3

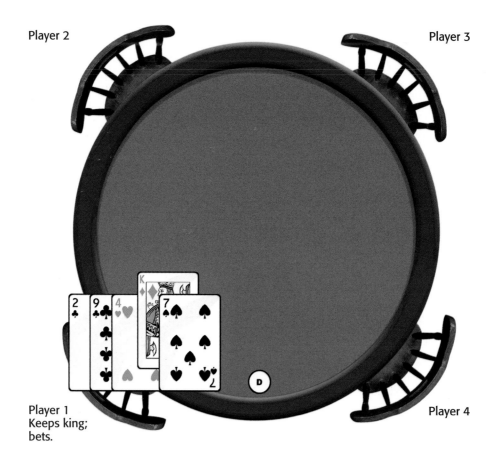

Player 1
Keeps king;
bets.

Player 4

PLAYER 2

Player 2 plans to hold the pair of jacks and calls (matches) player 1's bet. Player 2 also watches how other players bet to attempt to read the quality of their hands.

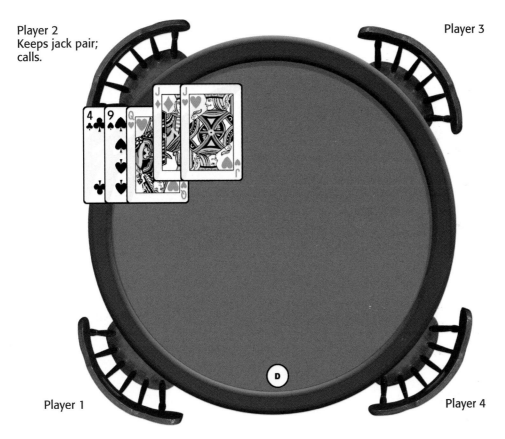

Player 2
Keeps jack pair;
calls.

Player 3

Player 1

Player 4

D

CONTINUED ON NEXT PAGE

PLAYER 3

Player 3 is holding a pair of aces, a good starting hand, but not the best (see "Draw Poker Chances" table). Player 3 calls the bet.

Player 2

Player 3
Keeps ace pair; calls.

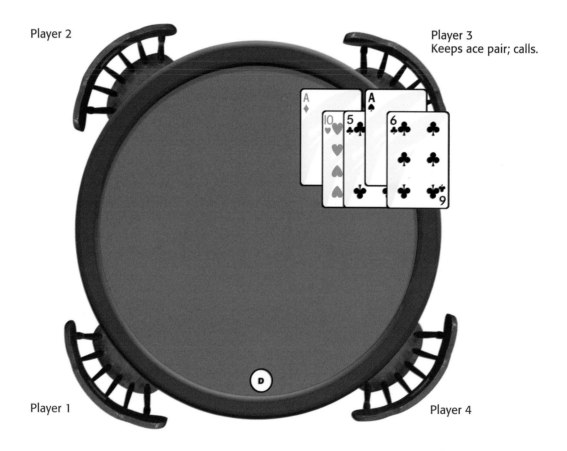

Player 1

Player 4

PLAYER 4

Player 4 has four cards of the same suit, a flush draw, and hopes to pick up a fifth spade on the draw. With a less than five chance of drawing a spade, player 4 calls.

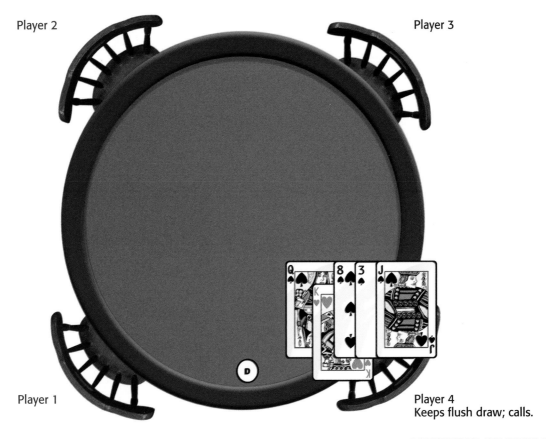

Player 2

Player 3

Player 1

Player 4
Keeps flush draw; calls.

CONTINUED ON NEXT PAGE

Example Game: Second Betting Interval

PLAYER 1

Player 1 keeps the king and discards four cards. The dealer deals four replacement cards that don't significantly improve the hand. Not knowing what the other players have, player 1 should fold. However, player 1 doesn't know what others will discard and whether a king-high will beat them, so stays in the game with a bet.

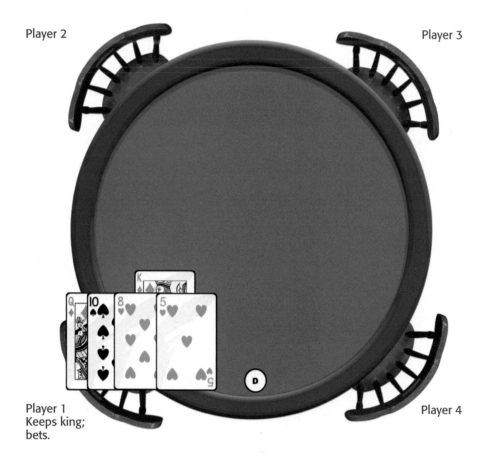

Player 2

Player 3

Player 1
Keeps king;
bets.

Player 4

PLAYER 2

Player 2 holds the pair of jacks and discards three cards. The draw gives player 1 a third jack that will beat two pairs. Player 2 raises the bet.

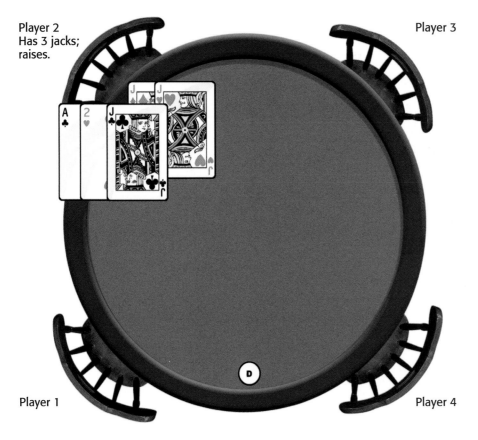

Player 2
Has 3 jacks;
raises.

Player 3

Player 1

Player 4

CONTINUED ON NEXT PAGE

Draw Poker
Betting *(continued)*

PLAYER 3

Player 3 holds the pair of aces and discards three, replaced by cards that don't help the hand. Knowing that the pair of aces will beat any other pair, but not three-of-a-kind, a straight, or a flush, player 3 calls the raise.

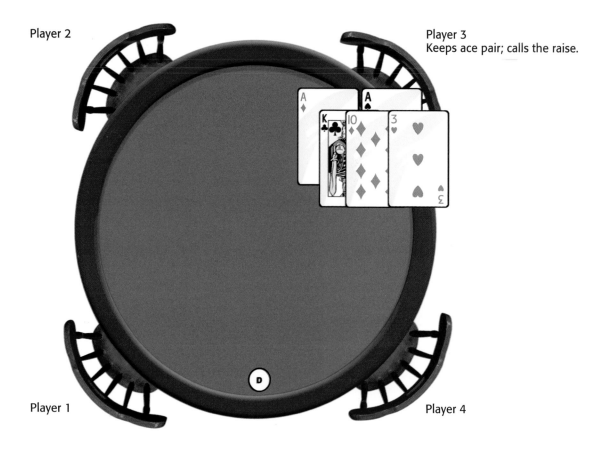

Player 2

Player 3
Keeps ace pair; calls the raise.

Player 1

Player 4

PLAYER 4

Player 4 holds a flush draw, needing one spade to complete the flush. The discarded card is replaced with a 7 ♥, making the hand a queen-high. In case this may be the highest hand, player 4 calls. To make the pot *right*, Player 1 must match Player 2's raise or fold.

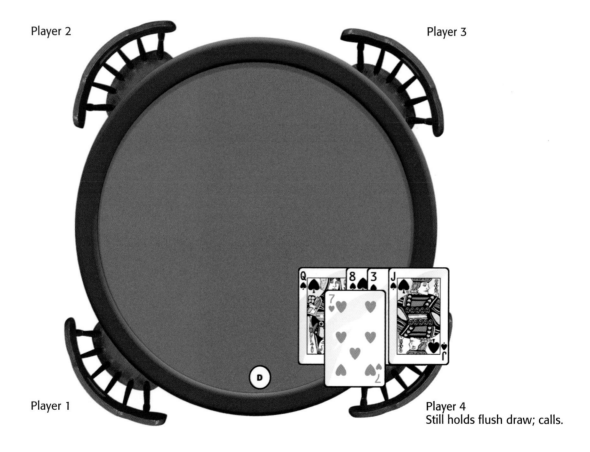

Player 2

Player 3

Player 1

Player 4
Still holds flush draw; calls.

The *showdown* is the presentation or facing of all active hands to determine the winner(s) of a pot based on game rules and hand rankings.

The showdown in standard draw poker comes after two betting intervals. Being an active player (one who hasn't folded) at showdown can be profitable—or expensive. The skills you develop playing draw poker, combined with the luck that is improved with those skills, can make you a winner at the showdown.

Example Game: Showdown

PLAYER 1

Player 1 shows a king-high hand, not a strong hand, but one that has won a few games. Player 1 realizes that he should have folded after the first betting interval when other players were discarding fewer cards.

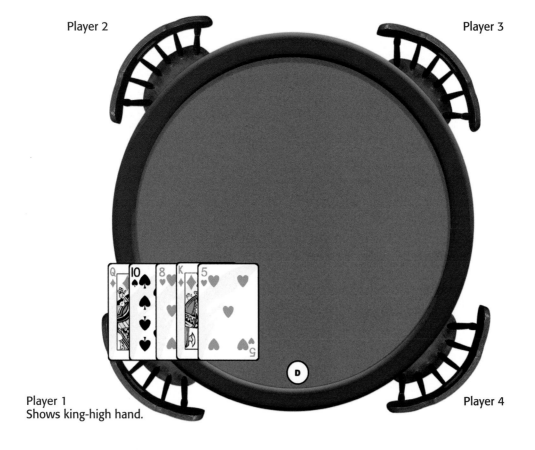

Player 2

Player 3

Player 1
Shows king-high hand.

Player 4

PLAYER 2

Player 2 shows three-of-a-kind, also known as a set or trips. It's a very good hand, but can be beaten by many other hands, so player 2 is glad that she bet conservatively.

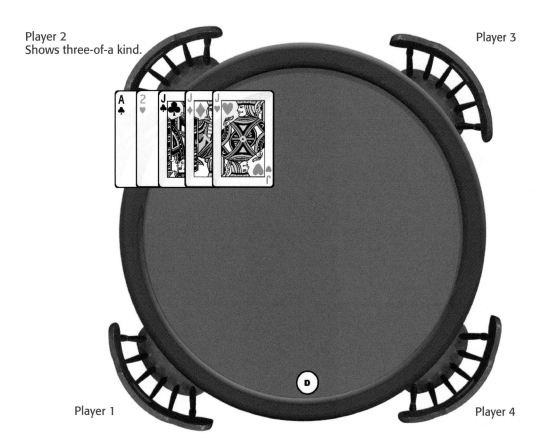

Player 2
Shows three-of-a kind.

Player 3

Player 1

Player 4

CONTINUED ON NEXT PAGE

PLAYER 3

Player 3 shows a pair of aces and everyone immediately realizes that the hand has been beaten by player 2's three-of-a-kind. Having the second-best hand at the table can be expensive, but player 3 also bet conservatively.

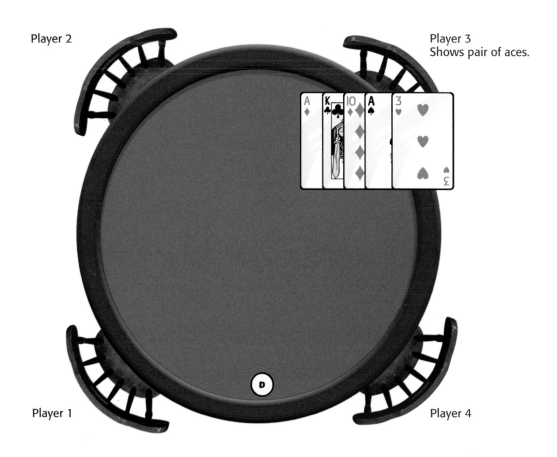

Player 2

Player 3
Shows pair of aces.

Player 1

Player 4

PLAYER 4

Sitting in the last position at the table, player 4 shows her cards to determine if she or player 2 is the winner of the pot. With a queen-high hand it is not only not a winner, it is the lowest ranking hand at the table. However, if she had drawn a spade hers would have beaten the best hand.

Player 2 wins!

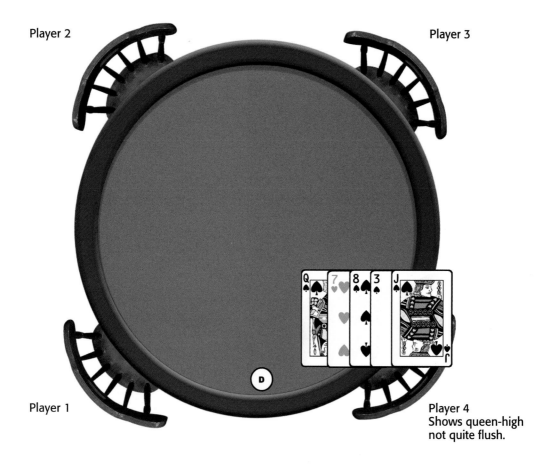

Player 2

Player 3

Player 1

Player 4
Shows queen-high
not quite flush.

Strategies for Winning Draw Poker

That's how the game of standard draw poker is played. But you don't just want to play—you want to *win!* Following are proven strategies and techniques for winning more chips at draw poker.

Ways to Win

DON'T BE AFRAID TO FOLD

If jacks or better are openers and you can't open, the better action is to fold if you have a poorer hand with little potential.

DON'T BE AFRAID TO RAISE

If you are the last player to bet (in other words, the dealer or the anchor to the right of the dealer) and you have a strong hand (a pair of aces or better), don't be afraid to raise the bet, as you probably have the best hand thus far.

KNOW THE ODDS AGAINST MATCHES

Poker is a game of chance and of odds. Know the odds against improving your hand when drawing three cards to your pair.

- Odds against any improvement: 2½-to-1
- Odds against making two pairs: 5-to-1
- Odds against making three-of-a-kind: 8-to-1
- Odds against making a full house: 97-to-1
- Odds against making four of a kind: 359-to-1

KNOW THE ODDS AGAINST STRAIGHTS

Odds against filling in a four-card straight when drawing one card:

- Odds against filling a straight open at both ends: 5-to-1
- Odds against filling a straight open at one end: 11-to-1
- Odds against filling a straight open (missing card) in the middle: 11-to-1

KNOW THE ODDS AGAINST FLUSHES

Odds against filling (completing) a flush:

- Odds against making a flush by drawing one card of the same suit: 4½-to-1
- Odds against making a flush by drawing two cards of the same suit: 23-to-1

Additional winning strategies are included in later chapters on playing draw poker at popular venues. For example, strategies for playing draw poker at home are found in Chapter 6, playing draw poker online is covered in Chapter 7, playing draw video poker is in Chapter 8, playing draw poker in casinos and card rooms is covered in Chapter 9, and playing draw poker in tournaments is described in Chapter 10.

Draw Poker Variations

There are many variations to standard draw poker. Some are sporadically popular, whereas other versions are regionally popular. A few are minor variations on common games. All are based on draw poker: five cards dealt face down with two or more betting intervals before the showdown.

Variations

DEALER'S CHOICE

Dealer's Choice is just that: whatever poker game the dealer wants to play. Whoever is the dealer selects and announces the game rules: Draw with Wild Cards, High-Low Draw, Straight Draw, Progressive Draw, Showdown, Pass-Out, Lowball, or some other variation. Shown is a Jokers-wild hand with three aces.

WILD CARDS

Some draw-poker games include wild cards, Jokers, or deuces that can represent any other card in the pack. If needed to make a straight, for example, a wild card can replace a specific card within the straight; for instance, A♠-Joker-Q♠-J♦-10♣, as shown in the photo. However, wild cards must be agreed on prior to the beginning of the game as the dealer announces "Draw poker, Jokers are wild." If wild cards are used, the standard rank of poker hands is changed, with the top hand being a five-of-a-kind (four of a kind plus the Joker) and a double-ace flush (flush with an ace and a Joker) being higher in rank than a flush.

HIGH-LOW DRAW

Draw poker also can be played for the lowest-ranking hand (*Low,* or *Lo*) or for both the highest- and lowest-ranking hands (*High-Low,* or *Hi-Lo*). At showdown, shown in the photo, the high hand (ace-high straight) and low hand (ace-low straight) split the pot.

STRAIGHT DRAW

Straight Draw is played exactly like standard draw poker except that a player may open on any hand—no minimum openers are required—and may draw up to five cards on the draw (shown).

PROGRESSIVE DRAW

If you're playing jacks or better to open and no one can open bidding, the hands are dealt again and a pair of queens or better is required to open (shown). If bidding is not opened, kings or better are needed to open the next deal; then aces or better are needed for the next deal. Once the game is opened by bidding, the following game reverts to jacks or better.

CONTINUED ON NEXT PAGE

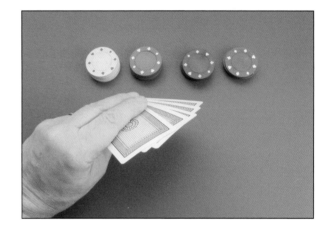

STRAIGHT POKER

Each player antes a set amount and is given five cards face down. There are betting intervals and a showdown, but no further cards drawn. You play what you are dealt.

JACKPOTS

Jackpots is simply standard draw poker requiring a pair of jacks or better to open. It is such a popular variation of draw poker that it often is considered the standard game. If the opening player folds before the showdown, he or she must show the opening pair.

PASS-OUT

In this simple variation on standard draw poker, no *checks* (bets of zero) are allowed. The player must bet or fold. In the illustration, the player has decided to fold on a poor hand.

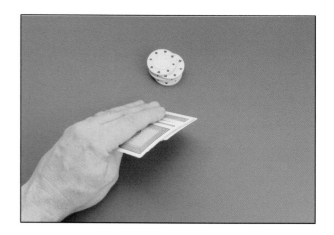

LOWBALL

Lowball is draw poker in reverse: the lowest hand wins the pot. In some games, a wild Joker, called the *bug*, is used as a missing card, a 5 in the photo. There are many other variations to this game, which often is played in casinos and card rooms.

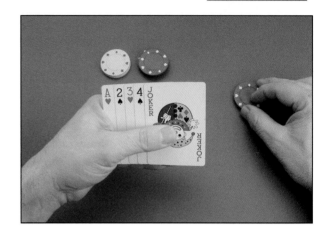

TRIPLE DRAW LOWBALL

Triple Draw is a new variation on Lowball with three draws and four betting rounds. Discarded cards are shown on the left. Because players have an additional chance to improve their hands, Triple Draw Lowball can have large pots.

SHOTGUN

Shotgun is draw poker with more betting intervals. The first betting interval comes after three cards are dealt to each player (such as the case in the photo). Another betting interval comes after the fourth card. Then a third interval comes once the fifth card is dealt. The draw is next, followed by a fourth and final betting interval. Otherwise, Shotgun is standard draw poker.

CONTINUED ON NEXT PAGE

POKE

Also known as Pokino, Poke is a more complex variation on draw poker. Only two players play. Five cards are dealt face down (shown). Up to three cards can be discarded. Then the hands are played out in *tricks,* or hands with one card contributed by each player and the highest card taking the trick. The results are scored similar to bridge. It's a fun variation.

KNOCK

If you enjoy Rummy, the poker variation called Knock may be fun to play. Five cards are dealt to each player, face down. The deck is placed in the middle of the table, face down, with the top card removed and placed beside the deck face up as the beginning of the discard stack. Each player selects either the face-up card or the top deck card and replaces it with one of their five cards in the face-up or discard stack. To keep a hand as is and not select from the discard stack, the player must knock once on the table. In showdown, the highest hand takes the pot. The pot includes the ante and one chip from each player who drops out.

WHISKEY

Considered the oldest form of poker, Whiskey (or Whisky) is a variation of draw poker. Each player is in turn dealt five cards face down. An additional hand, called the *widow,* is dealt face down to the table center. In rotation, a player may exchange a hand for the widow hand. If so, the new widow hand is placed face up and players may, in turn, select from it, replacing the card they take with a card from their hand (shown). At showdown, the highest hand takes the pot.

SPIT IN THE OCEAN

Spit in the Ocean is a draw poker game with dozens of its own variations (Pig in a Poke, Twin Beds, Klondike, Wild Widow, and so on). A *spit* is a card initially placed at the center of the table face up (shown here is the A♣) that any player can use to help form a hand. Two of the variations are today's most popular poker games: Texas Hold'em (see Chapter 4) and Omaha (see Chapter 5).

TIP

As the oldest form of American poker, draw poker is the simplest version. Many people prefer to start with draw poker to learn the basics of the game of poker, hand ranks, betting, and other skills that can be carried on to more complex poker games such as Stud, Hold'em, and Omaha. Because Draw is a relatively simple game, it is the basis for most video poker games (see Chapter 8). It's fun!

3

Stud Poker

Stud poker is a popular card game, especially on the East Coast of the U.S. and in many European countries. There are several variations of stud poker, with Seven-Card Stud the most popular by far. Seven-Card Stud is played at home but is more often found in card rooms, in some casinos, and online. Stud is considered a more difficult card game than standard draw poker because it involves remembering what cards have already been dealt in the hands. In addition, winning at stud requires reading everyone's hands more carefully to determine whether yours is the best. It's a fun game that is growing in popularity. Due to its greater prominence, this chapter focuses on Seven-Card Stud.

Stud poker is also known as *open poker* because some of the cards are dealt face up in front of each player. (Originally called stud-horse poker for unknown reasons, the term soon was shortened to stud poker.) Due to the greater skills required to analyze and bet on hands quickly, Stud is more popular with money players. In addition, Stud has more betting rounds than draw poker, so the pots are larger. The many variations of stud poker can make it a fascinating and profitable game.

The Game

Stud poker is played with a standard 52-card pack of playing cards. The object is to win the pot by holding at showdown a hand of *five* cards of higher rank than any other player. The standard ranks of poker hands are as presented in Chapter 1 (see page 12).

Once all players have agreed upon the game rules, each makes the initial bet, called the *ante,* into a common pot.

Two to ten players may simultaneously play stud poker, but seven players is the ideal number. In Seven-Card Stud, as shown in the figure (right side), two cards are dealt face down, one at a time, clockwise around the table to all active players. (In Five-Card Stud, as shown on the left column of the figure, only one card is dealt face down.) These are called the player's *hole* cards and are not seen by the other players until the end of the game unless the player folds the hand.

A third (*door*) card is dealt face up in front of each player, and the first betting interval begins with the player who shows the highest-ranking door card. Once the pot is balanced, a fourth card is dealt (*fourth street*), followed by betting. The process is repeated for the fifth and sixth cards (*fifth* and *sixth streets,* respectively), all face up. Finally, a seventh card is dealt to each player face down, and final betting begins.

Five-Card

Seven-Card

Betting

Because stud poker involves more betting rounds than draw poker, each player has more decisions to make. However, in each decision the underlying question is "What are the chances that my hand is the best at the table?" Knowing card, pot, and player odds is important.

In addition, stud players should know which cards are available to complete a hand—which cards are *live.* This means players should scrutinize all other board (face-up) cards as well as remember any board cards that have been *mucked* (discarded).

Seven-Card Stud typically is played with five betting intervals, after the dealing of the third, fourth, fifth, sixth, and final cards. Each interval might involve more than one round if any player raises the bet and other players are required to call or fold. Or they may *reraise* (raise another player's raise). Also, the pot must be *right*, meaning that all active players must have contributed an equal amount after every betting round before the game can continue.

After the final round of betting is the *showdown,* when all active players must show their cards for comparison of rank based on the game rules.

A stud poker hand combines up (seen) and down (unseen) cards. Therefore, reading hands quickly and determining odds are significant skills in successful play. This is especially true when analyzing your starting hand. In Seven-Card Stud, the starting hand consists of two hole cards and a *board* (face-up) card for each active player.

Good Hand Rankings

An advantage of playing stud is that you get to see many of your opponents' cards. For example, if your hole cards are a pair of jacks (called a *pocket pair*), you should look around the table to see whether any other jacks are showing before calculating the odds of being dealt one or more additional jacks. Observation and memory are important in stud poker.

Hand Rankings Table
A *straight flush* consists of five cards of the same suit, in sequence.
Four-of-a-kind (*quad*) is made up of four cards of the same rank, plus a fifth unrelated or odd card.
A *full house* consists of three-of-a-kind plus a pair of another kind or rank.
A *flush* is made up of five cards of the same suit, but not in sequence.
A *straight* consists of five cards in sequence, but not of the same suit.
Three-of-a-kind consists of three cards (*trips*) of the same rank, with two odd cards.
A *two-pair* hand is made up of two groups of cards of matching rank, with a fifth odd card.
A *one-pair* hand consists of two cards of matching rank, with three odd cards.
A *high-card* hand is none of the above, and its value is designated by the rank of the highest card (*ace high*) or lowest card (*deuce low*), depending on the rules of the game.

The best starting hand (third street) you can get in Seven-Card Stud is *three-of-a-kind*, also called a *set* or *trips*. The higher the rank, the better.

The second-best type of hand is one that contains *premium pairs:* AA, KK, QQ, JJ, or TT. If they are hole cards that others cannot see, so much the better. Also helpful is a *high kicker,* a single card of a high rank that will help you beat another player's pair if it has the same rank as yours.

Next in the list of good stud poker hands are middle and low pairs. Middle pairs are 99, 88, and 77. Low pairs are 66, 55, 44, 33, and 22.

With no pair among your starter cards, the next-best starting hands are three of the five cards needed to make a straight flush, such as Q♥, J♥, 10♥. You have four more cards to be dealt that might bring two more hearts to make a straight.

Flushes are of a higher rank than straights, so the next two best starting hands are flush draws followed by straight draws, three cards that could potentially become a flush or become a straight.

Finally, high cards among your three starting cards have lower ranking. Much depends on whether they will match up with one or more dealt cards.

Making Decisions

Which cards you will bet on depends on many factors, including which cards are showing in front of other players. You might have a pocket pair of a higher rank than any card on the board. Or you might see the mates to your pocket pair somewhere on the board, meaning you have no chance at making trips.

Also, the fewer the players, the better the chances that a lower-ranking starting hand can eventually win the pot. With some luck, a high-card hand can develop into a winning pair or trip.

The decisions you make on your starting hand and subsequent hands are based on odds. The following table gives you some useful odds for Seven-Card Stud.

Count the Odds Against You	
Making a flush from your first three suited cards	4.5-to-1
Making a straight from your first three sequenced cards	5-to-1
Being dealt a pair in the first three cards	5-to-1
Being dealt three suited cards	187-to-1
Being dealt three-of-a-kind (trips)	424-to-1

Poker is about betting. Five-Card Stud has four betting intervals, and the more popular Seven-Card Stud offers five opportunities to bet that you have the best hand at the showdown.

Stud is a board game. The face-up cards on the board are owned by the individual players. By comparison, Hold'em and Omaha are *flop* games in which the face-up cards on the table are communal, shared by all active players. That means Stud is a more intricate game that requires more reading of cards and players than flop games. Learning how to bet smart at Stud can be profitable.

Table Position

Where you sit at the table in relationship to other players is important. The chair doesn't matter, but the relative position in the betting order does. Shown is the numbered position relative to the dealer. Unfortunately, you have no control over the betting order during betting intervals. Here's who starts the betting at each interval:

- **Third street:** Starts with the *lowest* board card
- **Fourth street:** Starts with the *highest* board rank
- **Fifth street:** Starts with the *highest* board rank
- **Sixth street:** Starts with the *highest* board rank
- **River (final card):** Starts with the same player as sixth street

After the first-position player has had the opportunity to bet, the active player to the left can bet. The rotation is clockwise. Betting ends when all players are either equally invested in the pot or have folded.

Although you cannot change your betting position, knowing what position you have can help you make better betting decisions.

CONTINUED ON NEXT PAGE

Betting on Starting Hands (Third Street)

You have two hole cards and one board card, called the *door*. Based on the ranking of your starting hand (see the earlier "Stud Poker Starting Hands" section), you bet on your potential for holding the winning hand at the showdown.

Remember that you will select the best *five*-card hand from the *seven* you will be dealt—if you stay to the end.

EXAMPLE GAME: BETTING ON STARTING HANDS

Note: *Example games in this chapter are intended for basic instruction and do not reflect poker strategies.*

Player 1

Dealt an ace and four hole cards and an ace board or door card, player 1's starting hand is a pair of aces. Believing that he has the best hand at the table, he bets.

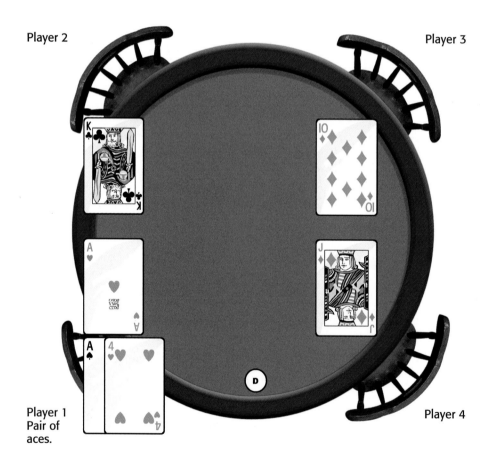

Player 2

Player 3

Player 1
Pair of
aces.

Player 4

Player 2

Player 2 is dealt a pair of sixes for hole cards and a king door card. The pair, called a *pocket pair,* is valuable as no other players know she has it. She calls (matches) player 1's bet.

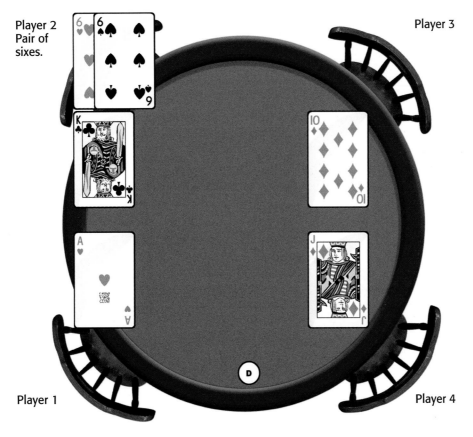

Player 2
Pair of
sixes.

Player 3

Player 1

Player 4

CONTINUED ON NEXT PAGE

Player 3

Player 3 is dealt two small unsuited cards and the door card doesn't help the hand. Odds are against him getting a better hand, but feeling "lucky" he calls.

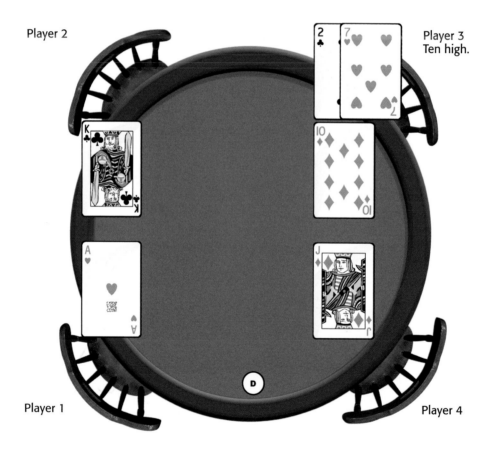

Player 2

Player 3
Ten high.

Player 1

Player 4

Player 4

Player 4 gets a jack and an eight unsuited in the hole plus a jack door card, making a pair of jacks. Knowing that this is a good (but not great) hand, player 4 calls.

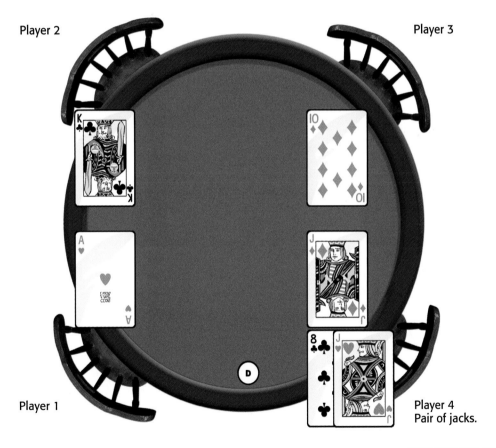

Player 2

Player 3

Player 1

Player 4
Pair of jacks.

CONTINUED ON NEXT PAGE

Betting on Fourth Street

You now have two hole cards and *two* board cards. If you remain active, you will be dealt three more cards, two up and one down (hidden from the view of the other players). As you determine your bet, make sure you know what cards are still live, or available. This is especially important if you are trying to draw a flush or a straight.

EXAMPLE GAME: BETTING ON FOURTH STREET

Player 1

The fourth card (fourth street) is a king, which doesn't help player 1 who is looking for another ace. However, he now has three hearts, which could become a flush. Player 1 bets.

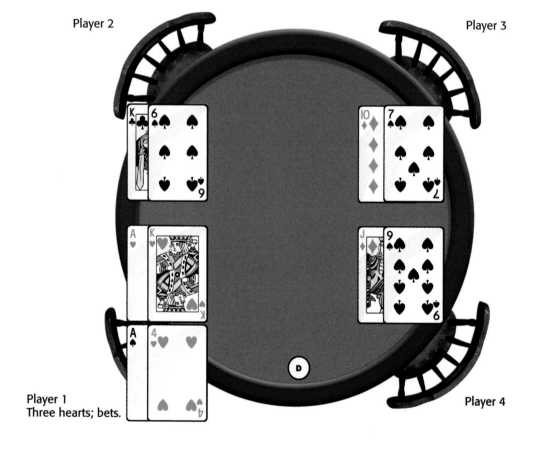

Player 2

Player 3

Player 1
Three hearts; bets.

Player 4

Player 2

Player 2's fourth card is a six! Unbeknownst to the other players, player 2 now has trips, three-of-a-kind. She raises the bet.

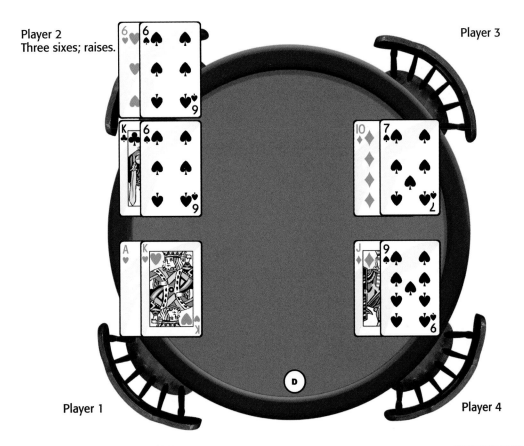

Player 2
Three sixes; raises.

Player 3

Player 1

Player 4

CONTINUED ON NEXT PAGE

Player 3

Player 3 is dealt a seven, making his hand a pair of sevens with a ten kicker. Not much, but, with hope for another seven and/or another ten, he calls the raise.

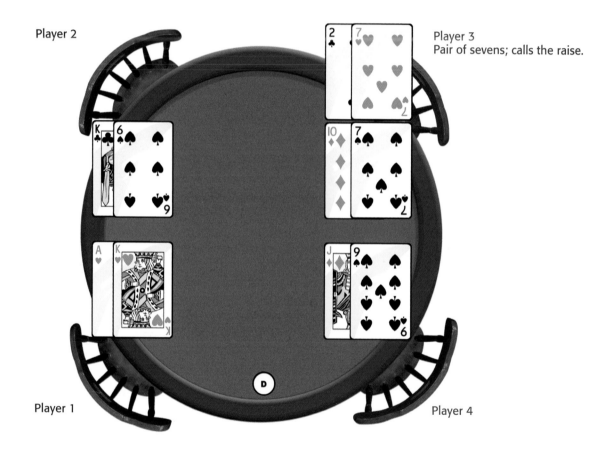

Player 2

Player 3
Pair of sevens; calls the raise.

Player 1

Player 4

Player 4

Player 4 gets a nine, which is no help to her pair of jacks, but does give her J-9-8. With the pair of jacks and fingers crossed, she calls the raise.

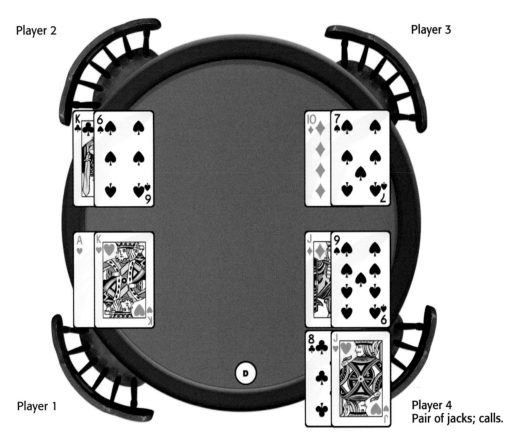

Player 2

Player 3

Player 1

Player 4
Pair of jacks; calls.

CONTINUED ON NEXT PAGE

Betting on Fifth Street

The dealer deals another up-card to each player. Each hand is now two hole cards and *three* board cards. You might already have a winning hand of five, or you might need one or even two more cards to make a hand. In many Seven-Card Stud games, the minimum bet doubles on fifth street, so be sure you have a good hand before continuing.

EXAMPLE GAME: BETTING ON FIFTH STREET

Player 1

Player 1 is dealt another king, making his hand two pair, aces and kings. No other aces are showing on the board, but one king is showing, meaning that there may be up to two aces and one more king among the cards to be dealt. Player 1 bets.

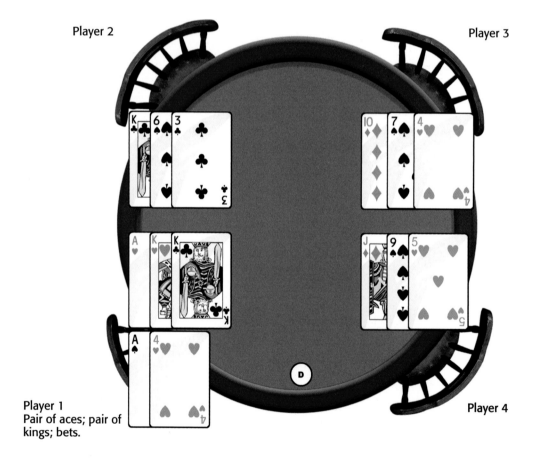

Player 2

Player 3

Player 1
Pair of aces; pair of
kings; bets.

Player 4

Player 2

The fifth card for player 2 is a three, no help to her three sixes. But, knowing that she has two more cards to be dealt, a full house looks like a possibility. She raises player 1's bet.

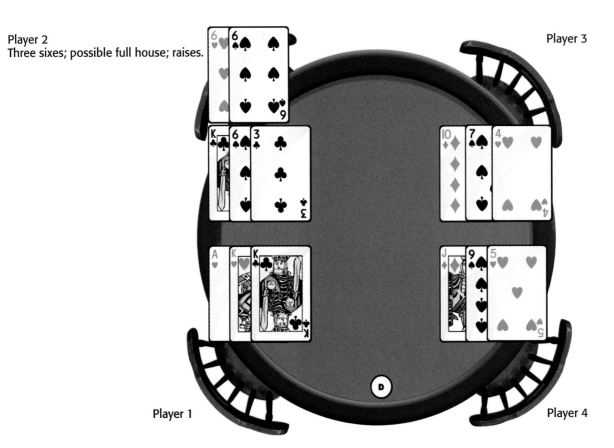

Player 2
Three sixes; possible full house; raises.

Player 3

Player 1

Player 4

CONTINUED ON NEXT PAGE

Player 3

Player 3 is dealt a four. Without a good hand and without any chance of getting a good hand within the next two cards, player 3 folds.

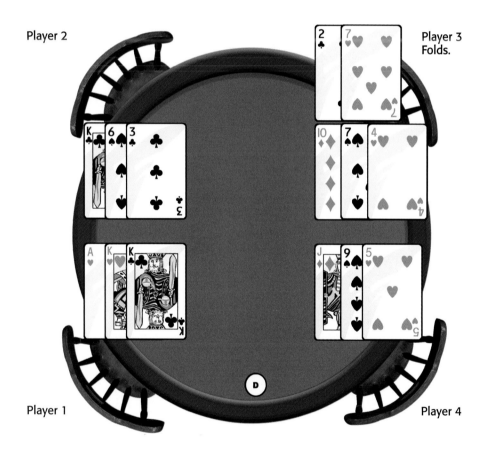

Player 2

Player 3
Folds.

Player 1

Player 4

Player 4

Player 4 is dealt a five on fifth street, so her hand is still a pair of jacks. Recognizing that player 1 has a pair of kings showing—and who knows what else in his hand—player 4 folds.

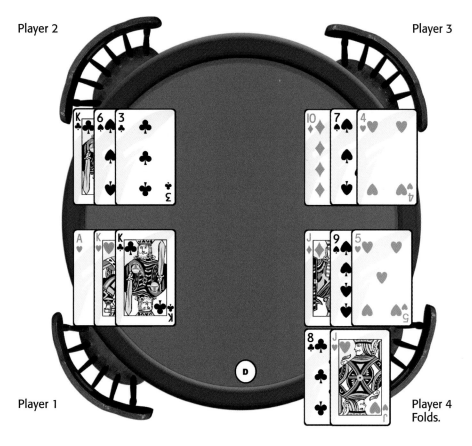

Player 2

Player 3

Player 1

Player 4
Folds.

CONTINUED ON NEXT PAGE

Betting on Sixth Street

Your hand—and everyone else's—is two hole cards and *four* board cards. You should have a winning hand by now, or you should have folded. This sixth card might give you a full house or a higher flush or straight than you had. Bet accordingly.

EXAMPLE GAME: BETTING ON SIXTH STREET

Player 1

Dealt an eight, player 1 still has two pair. Because player 2's board cards don't look like a good hand, player 1 bets that he has the best hand.

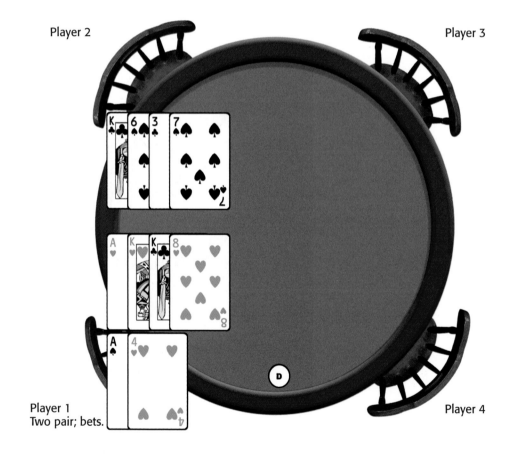

Player 2

Player 3

Player 1
Two pair; bets.

Player 4

Player 2

Player 2's next board card is a seven, no help to her three sixes. As player 1 has three hearts on the board—a possible flush—she decides to call the bet.

Player 2
Three-of-a-kind; possible flush;
possible full house; calls.

Player 3

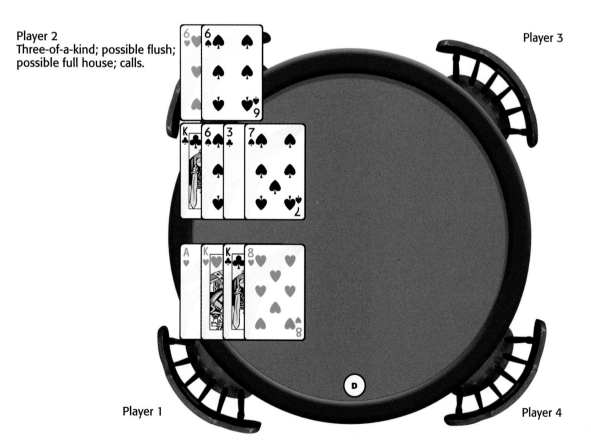

Player 1

Player 4

CONTINUED ON NEXT PAGE

Betting on the River

The *river* card is the final card dealt in Seven-Card Stud and it comes to you face *down.* Smart players fold before the river if they don't already have what they believe is the best hand at the table (although they might try to steal the pot, a concept covered under the later "Strategies for Winning Stud Poker" section).

The river card can enhance an already top hand, ensuring that it will be *the* winner. Of course, it can also do the same for one of your opponents. If you don't believe that you have the winning hand based on the five showing cards and the betting patterns of other players, consider folding. The river is often where players raise and reraise on winning hands—or on a bluff. Having the second-best hand can be costly.

EXAMPLE GAME: BETTING ON THE RIVER

Player 1

The final card, the river, is dealt face down to the two remaining players. Player 1 gets a three and, more importantly, a heart. He now has an ace-high heart flush (A-K-8-4-3). He bets.

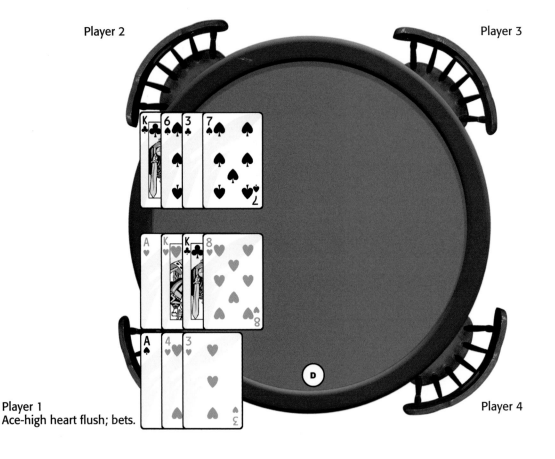

Player 2

Player 3

Player 1
Ace-high heart flush; bets.

Player 4

Player 2

Player 2's final card is a queen. It doesn't help her three sixes, nor does she have a straight or a flush. Hoping that player 1 has two pair and not three kings, she calls.

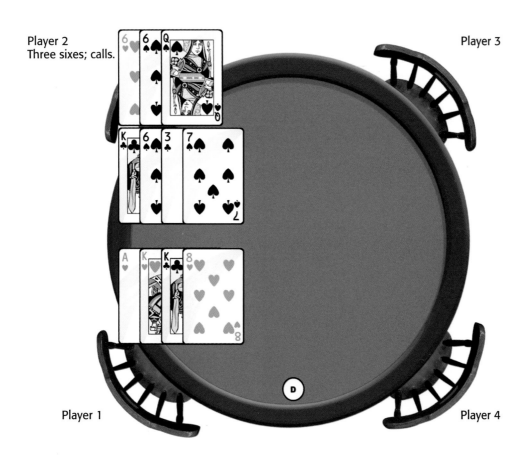

Player 2
Three sixes; calls.

Player 3

Player 1

Player 4

The showdown is the presentation or facing of all active hands to determine the winner(s) of a pot based on game rules and hand rankings.

The showdown in Seven-Card Stud comes after seven cards are dealt and up to five betting intervals are complete.

Example Game: Showdown

PLAYER 1

Player 1 lays them down: an ace-high heart flush. Will it be the best hand at the table? You already know, but player 1 won't until showdown.

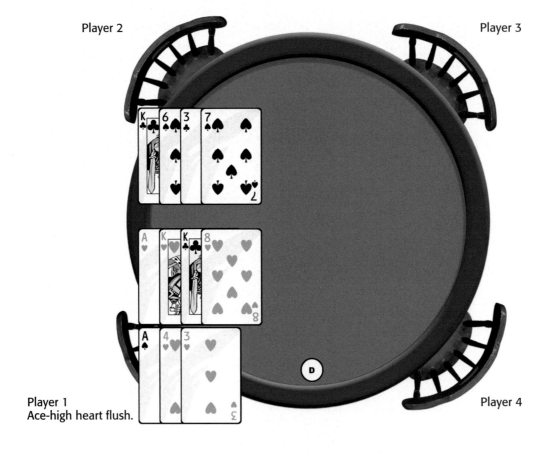

Player 2

Player 3

Player 1
Ace-high heart flush.

Player 4

PLAYER 2

Player 2 shows three sixes with a king and a queen.

Player 1 wins!

However, if player 1 had not been dealt a heart on the river, player 2 would have won. That's poker!

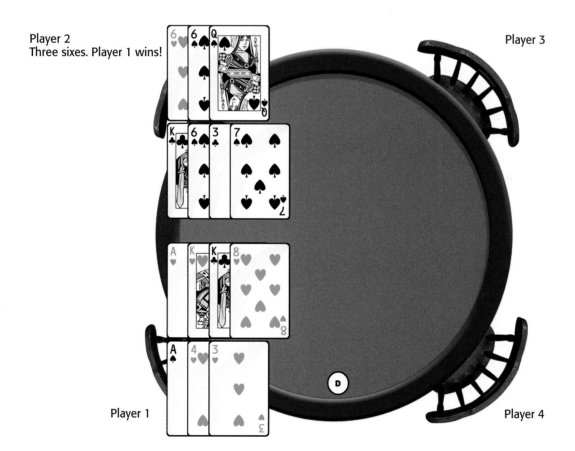

Player 2
Three sixes. Player 1 wins!

Player 3

Player 1

Player 4

Strategies for Winning Stud Poker

Stud poker is a powerful game that requires more skill than draw and many other forms of poker. That means smart players win more. Here are numerous proven strategies for winning at Seven-Card Stud. Many can be applied to winning Five-Card Stud and other versions of stud poker.

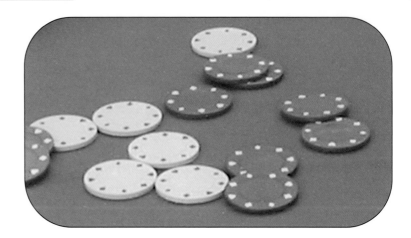

Strategies

KEEP TRACK OF THE LIVE CARDS

Seven-Card Stud is a game of live (available) cards. If your memory is good—or at least better than your opponents'—you can improve your chances of winning by knowing what cards are probably still in the deck and which have been folded. If your memory isn't so good, rely on your eyes to see whether the five or ten of clubs you need for your straight flush is already on the board, shown.

TIP

If you are playing stud poker online, there are various software programs that can help you keep track of the live or available cards (see Appendix B). For example, PokerPal and PokerInspector graphically illustrate a 52-card deck and indicate which cards have not been shown yet. They cannot tell you what cards have been dealt to players face down, but can help you determine with greater accuracy whether the card(s) you need may be available.

FORCE COMPETITORS TO CALL A RAISE

If you hold a strong hand, such as four kings (shown), but up-cards show a weak hand, raise to force competitors to bet more against your seemingly weak hand.

BACK *THE* WINNER

Make sure you realize the difference between a winning hand and *the* winning hand. A winning hand—a full house, for example—may still be beaten by four-of-a-kind or a straight flush. Studying your opponents' cards might tell you that a higher winning hand than yours is possible.

CONTINUED ON NEXT PAGE

full house   straight flush

DON'T CHASE A BAD HAND

All players, even the pros, sometimes make the wrong decision. And they know it once it is made. They invest chips in a hand that has a very low chance of winning, hoping that something miraculous will happen. It doesn't. The only thing worse is not stopping once you know you are *chasing* (betting on) a bad hand.

DON'T GIVE AWAY FREE CARDS

If you know that you have the strongest hand, bet or raise. Not only will it bring more chips into the pot, but it also will keep opponents from *checking,* or betting zero. Such a bet might get them another card dealt, and it might be the exact one they need in order to beat your hand. In the illustration, your three aces may get beaten by the other player's possible flush.

Additional winning strategies are included in later chapters on playing stud poker at popular venues.

Seven-Card Stud is the most popular version of the classic stud poker game. However, there are many other stud games that are fun and profitable to play. Some are obviously social games for home play, but many can be found in casinos and card rooms. Following are some popular variations, including Five-Card Stud and Seven-Stud/8 (pronounced "seven-stud split eight").

Play Poker Variations

FIVE-CARD STUD

Five-Card Stud is a predecessor of Seven-Card Stud. The primary differences are that only five cards are dealt—one down and four up—and there are four betting intervals instead of five. Five-Card Stud is popular as a home game.

SEVEN-STUD/8

For an even more complex game than Seven-Card Stud, try it as a hi-lo game requiring eights or lower to qualify for the low hand. The highest and lowest hands split the pot. Because some players are playing for high hands and others for low hands, the pots can get large.

In some casinos and card rooms, Seven-Stud/8 is the most popular game, especially with professional and semi-professional players. Pots can become quite large. Because there may be two winners (or one big winner), more players tend to stay in the game longer. If you're considering this game, find an online game first to learn the skills to win consistently.

CONTINUED ON NEXT PAGE

TIP

Because Five-Card Stud is simpler to learn and has fewer betting rounds than Seven-Card Stud, many new players begin with this variation. However, nearly all gaming casinos and card rooms prefer Seven-Card Stud. Fortunately, the transition from Five- to Seven-Card Stud is relatively easy, with betting the primary difference.

WILD CARDS

Some stud poker games include wild cards, such as Jokers or deuces, that can represent any other card in the pack. If a wild card is needed to make a straight, for example, it can replace a specific card within a straight: Joker-9-8-7-6 with the Joker standing in for the ten. However, wild cards must be agreed upon prior to the beginning of the game, as the dealer announces "Seven-Card Stud, Jokers are wild." If wild cards are used, the standard rank of poker hands is changed. The top hand is five-of-a-kind, and a double-ace flush is higher in rank than a flush.

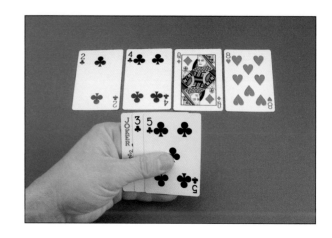

ENGLISH

English Seven-Card Stud deals two hole cards and three board cards, as standard Five-Card Stud does, with betting rounds. Each player can then discard and draw a card, and then bet again. The discard-draw-bet is repeated, so a player can be dealt up to seven cards, five of which can make a hand. A player who stands pat for the first draw must stand pat for the second.

DR. PEPPER

Named for the soda pop, this game is played like Seven-Card Stud except that all tens, fours, and deuces are wild and can represent any other card in the deck.

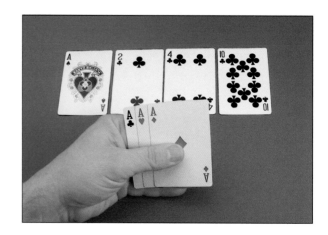

WOOLWORTH

Named for the department store, this variant is played like Seven-Card Stud except that all fives and tens are wild.

PASS-OUT STUD

A simple variation on Five- and Seven-Card Stud, with no checks (bets of zero) allowed. The player must bet, call, or fold.

TWO-LEG STUD

Played like Five- and Seven-Card Stud, but the winner can take only every other pot he or she wins, not consecutive pots. Pots accumulate until won.

CONTINUED ON NEXT PAGE

SEVEN-CARD FLIP

Similar to Seven-Card Stud, four cards initially are dealt face down to each player. The player can choose two of them to *flip,* or turn face up. Betting begins, followed by three up cards, each with a betting interval, before the showdown.

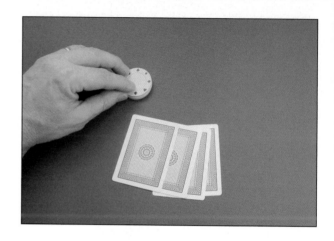

EIGHT-CARD STUD

An extension of Seven-Card Stud, this game adds a final card and betting interval at the end. The eighth card can be either up or down depending on what is agreed before the game. A hand is limited to the best five of the eight cards.

LOWBALL STUD

This game can be played with five or seven cards, but only five are chosen as the best hand. Best in this case is the lowest-ranking hand (see Chapter 1). The seven-card version is known as *Razz* and is very popular in some casinos and card rooms. Shown is a five-low hand with the highest card a five.

BASEBALL

A variation of Seven-Card Stud, Baseball is fun—if you can remember the rules. A 3-spot board card strikes out the player. A 4-spot board card gets an extra card (a walk). Threes and fours as hole cards are okay. Nines are wild. Batter up!

MEXICAN STUD

Only one down (hole) card is allowed at a time in Mexican Stud, a variation of Five-Card Stud. The first two cards are dealt face down to each player, who then turns up either one of them. Bets begin with the player holding the highest up (board) card. A third card is dealt face down, and the player can turn it or the other down card up, followed by another betting interval. The fourth and fifth cards also are dealt down and the player must turn each one—or the hole card—up. There is more betting before the showdown.

CHICAGO

A variation of Seven-Card Stud, Chicago splits the pot between the highest hand and the holder of the highest spade in the hole. If no one has a spade, high hand wins the pot.

Hold'em Poker

The world's most popular poker game is Texas Hold'em. It is played in Lubbock, Lima, London, and Los Angeles. In fact, online Hold'em games have tables with players from these and many other locations around the world simultaneously. Its wide and growing popularity is because the game is deceptively simple to learn but very difficult to play well against professionals. Every player wants to learn more—and someday buy a chair at the biggest poker challenge, the televised World Series of Poker Main Event, where the game is no-limit Hold'em.

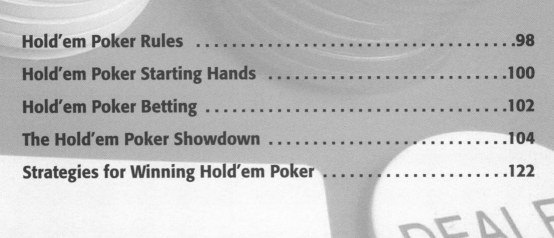

Hold'em Poker Rules

Texas Hold'em, commonly known as Hold'em or Holdem, is a simple game that can be learned quickly but takes a lifetime to master. Meantime, players find low-stakes and even free games to help them develop their skills and win more pots.

The Game

Texas Hold'em poker is played with a standard 52-card pack of playing cards. The object is to win the pot by holding the highest-ranking hand at the show-down. Up to *seven* cards are available to each active player (shown). Each player's hand is composed of the best *five* cards from among their two hole cards and the five board, or community, cards. The standard ranks of poker hands are as presented in Chapter 1 (see page 12).

Once the game rules are agreed upon, the first two players on the dealer's left are asked to make an initial *blind* bet before cards are dealt. Typically, the first player to the dealer's left makes a *small blind* bet and the next player makes the *big blind* bet. Subsequent players may call, raise, or fold.

Two to 20 players may simultaneously play Hold'em, but most games are limited to 10 players due to the size of the deck.

FAQ

How does Hold'em differ from stud poker?
Hold'em differs from stud poker in many important ways. First, the face-up board cards in Hold'em are community cards, shared by all players. That means the starting hand of two hole cards is more important to a Hold'em player. In addition, a player's position in the betting sequence is more important. It changes with each hand, circulating around the table. The betting sequence in stud depends on the ranking of board cards, which is an uncontrollable factor.

Betting Periods

There are typically four betting periods in a game of Hold'em. The dealer, identified by a chip-like button with *D* or *Dealer* on it, deals two cards to each active player, one card at a time and face down. These are the players' starting hands, or *hole* cards. A period of betting begins. Once the pot is balanced, three cards are dealt face up in the center of the table; this is called the *flop,* community cards that all players share. A second round of betting occurs.

The dealer then deals a fourth card, called *fourth street* or *the turn,* face up, and a third betting period begins. The betting might include bets, checks, calls, raises, and folds, ending when all active players are equally invested in the pot.

The fifth card, called *fifth street* or the *river* card, then is dealt face up with the other board cards, and a final period of betting occurs.

Once the pot is right, all active players show their final hands—five cards from the two hole and five board cards—at the showdown. The best hand is selected by the dealer or mutual agreement based on the game rules and hand rankings. In case of a tie, the pot is split.

Professional Hold'em players often prefer no-limit games where the betting is limited to your stake. Most home and semi-pro players prefer to play games with fixed betting limits. The most common is *two-tiered limits.* A 10/20 game, for example, limits an individual bet to $10 for the first two betting periods and doubles it to $20 for the last two betting periods. With three or four raises allowed during each round, a 10/20 pot can grow to $1,000 or more.

Unless otherwise agreed, the small blind bet is half the minimum, $5 in this example, and the big blind bet is the amount of the limit, $10 in this example. Limit games also have a limit, or *cap,* on the number of raises allowed in each betting round, typically three or four.

For additional information on betting in Hold'em, see "Hold'em Poker Betting," later in this chapter.

Hold'em Poker Starting Hands

Because the first two hole cards are your starting hand and the only cards you have that others can't see, it is vital to "know when to hold'em."

Getting Off to a Good Start

CHECK YOUR HAND

There are 169 possible two-card Hold'em starting hands in a deck. The better starting hands are paired cards (both of the same rank) or close suited cards (both of the same suit). Among paired cards, the higher the rank the better; AA is better than KK. Among suited cards, adjacent or connected cards are better than unconnected; for example, 8♠-7♠ is better than 10♠-7♠.

The table on the facing page shows the relative values of all possible Hold'em starting hands, both suited and unsuited.

KNOW YOUR POSITION

Some starting cards are playable only in later positions, depending on what has been shown and how other players bet. Position is your seating position at the table relative to the dealer. The small blind (SB), big blind (BB), and *under-the-gun* (next) positions are early; the dealer and *cutoff* (just before the dealer) are late; all others are middle positions; and the position depends on how many players are active.

Position is important because players in later positions can better estimate hand strengths based on the betting of prior players, an unknown for those in early positions. The best rule is to play only the best starting hands in the early positions and allow second-best hands in later positions once you know how others are betting.

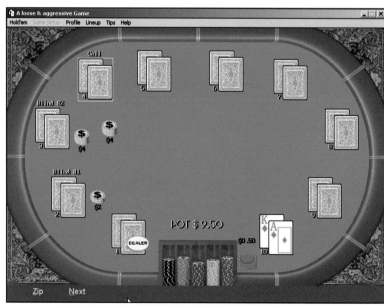

Hold'em Starting Hand Chart

The chart shown offers a guideline for selecting starting hands in Hold'em poker. AA means two aces; AKs means an ace and a king of the same suit. The dark green starting hands (AA, KK) should be played in any table position. The lighter green pairs (QQ, JJ, etc.) are played at any table position except by the tightest (most conservative) players. The dark blue (suited) and dark pink (unsuited) starting hands are played from middle and late positions, depending on the player's risk comfort and the size of the bets. The light blue (suited) and pink (unsuited) starting hands should only be played in low-limit games at late table positions, depending on the player's risk comfort.

This chart is a beginning point for most Hold'em players in determining which starting hands to play. With experience, you will memorize this table to use as a guideline to help make better plays.

AA	AKs	AQs	AJs	ATs	A9s	A8s	A7s	A6s	A5s	A4s	A3s	A2s
AK	KK	KQs	KJs	KTs	K9s	K8s	K7s	K6s	K5s	K4s	K3s	K2s
AQ	KQ	QQ	QJs	QTs	Q9s	Q8s	Q7s	Q6s	Q5s	Q4s	Q3s	Q2s
AJ	KJ	QJ	JJ	JTs	J9s	J8s	J7s	J6s	J5s	J4s	J3s	J2s
AT	KT	QT	JT	TT	T9s	T8s	T7s	T6s	T5s	T4s	T3s	T2s
A9	K9	Q9	J9	T9	99	98s	97s	96s	95s	94s	93s	92s
A8	K8	Q8	J8	T8	98	88	87s	86s	85s	84s	83s	82s
A7	K7	Q7	J7	T7	97	87	77	76s	75s	74s	73s	72s
A6	K6	Q6	J6	T6	96	86	76	66	65s	64s	63s	62s
A5	K5	Q5	J5	T5	95	85	75	65	55	54s	53s	52s
A4	K4	Q4	J4	T4	94	84	74	64	54	44	43s	42s
A3	K3	Q3	J3	T3	93	83	73	63	53	43	33	32s
A2	K2	Q2	J2	T2	92	82	72	62	52	42	32	22

Hold'em Poker Betting

Texas Hold'em has four betting periods: before the flop, after the flop, after the turn card, and after the river card. The showdown follows.

BET THE PRE-FLOP

Based on the quality of their starting hand and their position at the table, players make the first bet of the game, called the *pre-flop bet*. The bet is based on the limit (if any) and the relative strength of the opening cards and position. The illustration shows an AQ suited, a very good starting hand from most table positions. As the chart on the preceding page illustrates, a common opening hand might be playable in late positions if others haven't bet heavily, but is not worth a bet if the player is in one of the early positions.

BET THE POST-FLOP

With five cards (two hole cards and three shared board cards), players now can bet, check (bet zero), call, or fold based on the possibility that they will have the best hand or be the only player at the showdown.

In the figure, the player has four suited cards, a flush draw or an inside straight flush depending on what cards come next. A fifth spade among the final two cards would give him a flush (A♠-Q♠-K♠-T♠-4♠); a king of spades would give him a straight flush (A♠-K♠-Q♠-J♠-T♠), also known as a Royal Flush. In addition, a king of another suit would give him a straight. There are many things to consider.

In split-limit games (10/20, for example), this is the last opportunity to play a weak hand at little or no additional cost. If everyone checks or if the minimum bet is low enough, a weak hand could get a free or cheap turn card that might make the difference. However, if you determine that even a good turn card won't help your hand, it's probably time to fold rather than bet.

Remember that it costs nothing to check if everyone else has checked.

BET THE TURN

Players now see six of seven cards, but only two of them (the hole cards) are unknown to the other players. By watching the betting and using some advanced techniques (see the section "Strategies for Winning Hold'em Poker"), smart Hold'em players might accurately guess what other players are holding.

In the figure, a 2♥ doesn't help the hand, so the player calls the previous bet, knowing he has one more card, the river, in which to get a straight flush, a flush, or a straight.

Remember that stated-limit Hold'em games ($10/$20) double the minimum bet after the turn and river cards are dealt. Professional players know that the odds are great that if they don't have a winning hand by now, the river card won't give it to them. In low-stakes games (5¢/10¢), players often play their opening hands longer.

BET THE RIVER

All seven cards have been dealt. Five of the cards, the *board* or *community hand,* are for every player's use—with their two hole cards—in making the best hand. Expect some of the remaining players to fold and others to begin raising and reraising. Those who fold typically didn't get a river card that would fill a straight or flush, or believe their hand isn't worth investing any more chips in. Most raisers believe that they are the odds-on winner of the game and will bet accordingly. Only one (although maybe more in the case of a tie) will be the actual winner.

In the figure, the board was dealt a K♠ as the river card. The player now has a straight flush (A♠-K♠-Q♠-J♠-T♠). Actually, because the straight flush includes the ace it is a Royal Flush, a very rare hand.

Knowing how to play Hold'em well can earn you more games—and more chips—at the showdown.

TIP

When deciding how much to bet, leave emotion and ego out of the equation. The cards don't care. Bet because you believe that you hold the best hand at the table. Also consider the odds of improving your hand with the final card, the river.

The Hold'em Poker Showdown

The showdown is the presentation or facing of all active hands to determine the winner(s) of a pot based on game rules and hand rankings. The showdown in Texas Hold'em comes after seven cards are dealt and four betting intervals are complete.

Let's look at a full game to learn how players got to the showdown.

Example Game: Starting Hand

Note: *Example games in this chapter are intended for basic instruction and do not reflect poker strategies.*

PLAYER 1

Player 1 is dealt an ace and king of the same suit, spades. Referring to the Hold'em Starting Hand Chart (see page 101), this is an excellent hand from most any table position. Player 1 is in an early (first position), and bets.

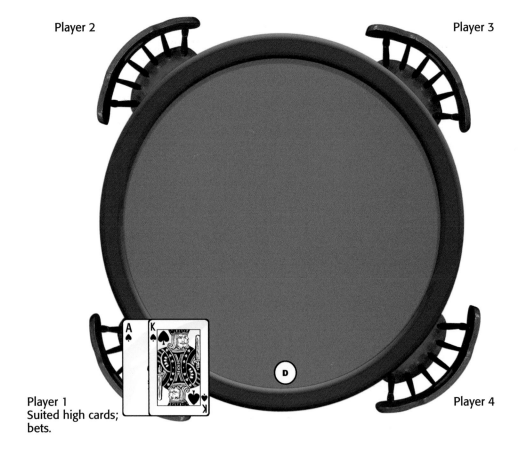

Player 2

Player 3

Player 1
Suited high cards;
bets.

Player 4

PLAYER 2

Player 2 is dealt a pair of fives, a good starting hand for middle and later positions. Player 2 calls (matches) player 1's initial bet.

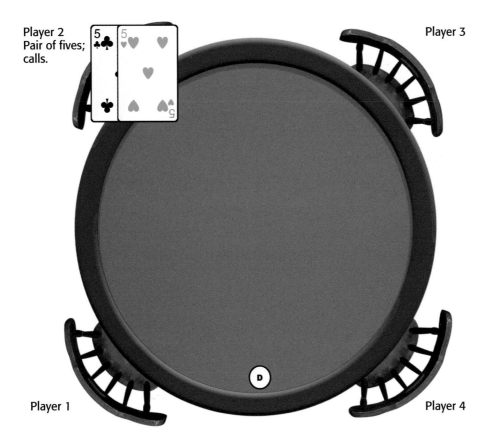

Player 2
Pair of fives;
calls.

Player 3

Player 1

Player 4

CONTINUED ON NEXT PAGE

PLAYER 3

In mid- to late-position, player 3 is dealt a poor hand, eight and four unsuited. In many games, player 3 should fold. As this is a friendly game, played for peppermints, player 3 calls.

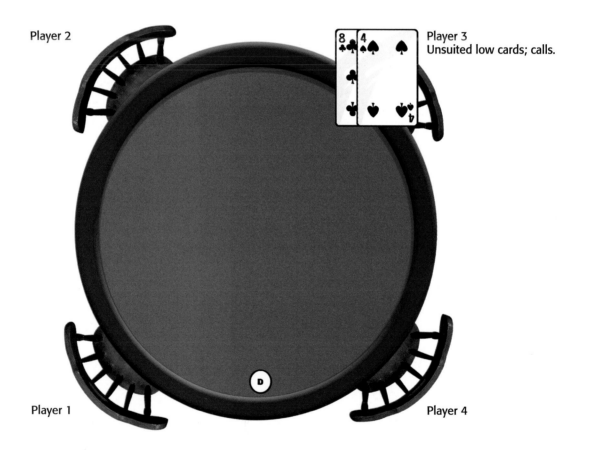

Player 2

Player 3
Unsuited low cards; calls.

Player 1

Player 4

PLAYER 4

In the last table position, player 4 can watch others bet before deciding whether her hand is worth an initial bet. King-ten suited is a very good starting hand, so she calls. If desired, player 4 may raise (increase the bet), requiring the other three players to either call the raise or fold.

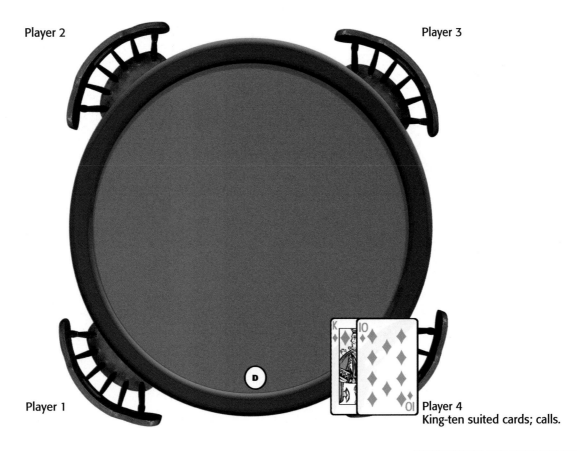

Player 2

Player 3

Player 1

Player 4
King-ten suited cards; calls.

CONTINUED ON NEXT PAGE

Example Game: Flop

PLAYER 1

All players are still in the game at the flop when three community (shared) or board cards are dealt. The flop is a 4♦-A♥-J♦. Player 1 now has a pair of aces and bets.

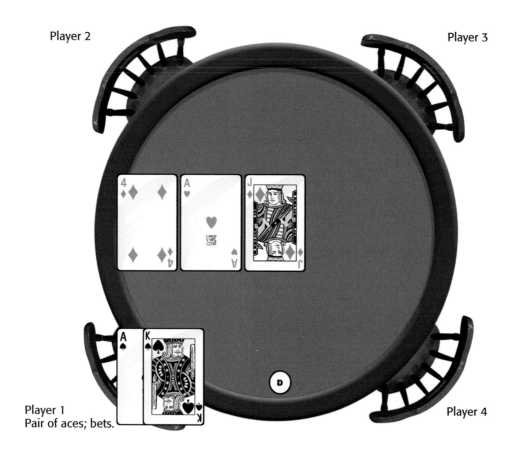

Player 2

Player 3

Player 1
Pair of aces; bets.

Player 4

PLAYER 2

The flop doesn't help player 2. Hoping for another 5 on the turn and/or river, player 2 calls player 1's bet.

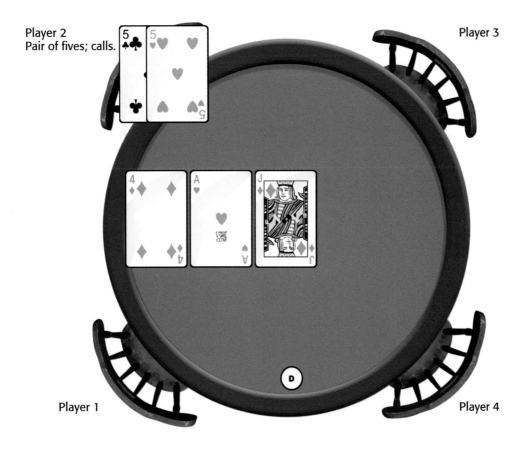

Player 2
Pair of fives; calls.

Player 3

Player 1

Player 4

CONTINUED ON NEXT PAGE

PLAYER 3

After the flop, player 3 has a pair of fours. He watches other players and their bets to guess whether anyone else may be able to beat his fours. If any other player has a single ace or jack as hole cards, they have a pair that will beat him. However, he throws caution to the wind and calls the bet with peppermints.

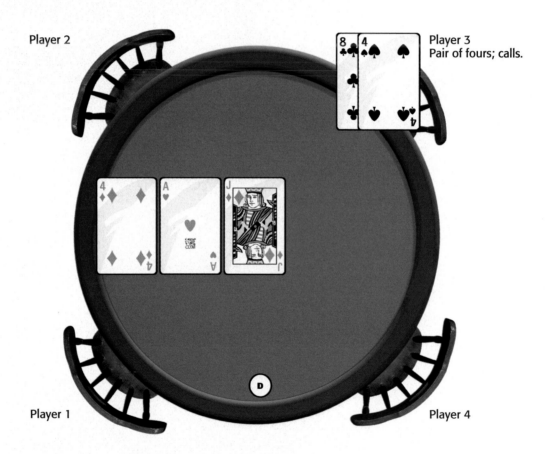

Player 2

Player 3
Pair of fours; calls.

Player 1

Player 4

PLAYER 4

Player 4, with two diamonds, picks up two more diamonds (4♦-J♦) on the flop. Player 4 needs a fifth diamond in the next two cards (turn and river) to get a flush, so she is "drawing" to a flush.

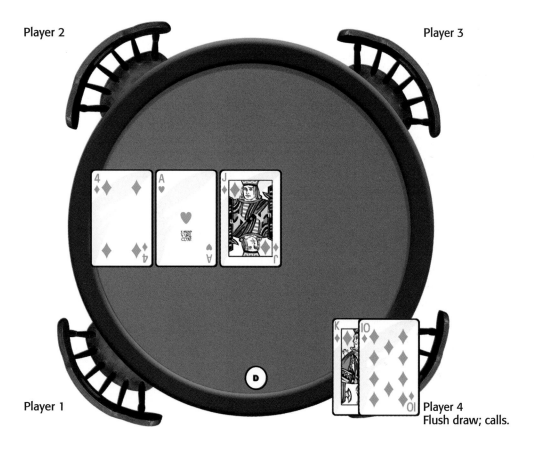

Player 2

Player 3

Player 1

Player 4
Flush draw; calls.

CONTINUED ON NEXT PAGE

Example Game: Turn

PLAYER 1

The turn card, also known as sixth street, is a seven of spades, giving player 1 a third spade. However, with only one more card coming, the river, he knows he cannot draw to a flush. His best hand is still a pair of aces. Player 1 bets.

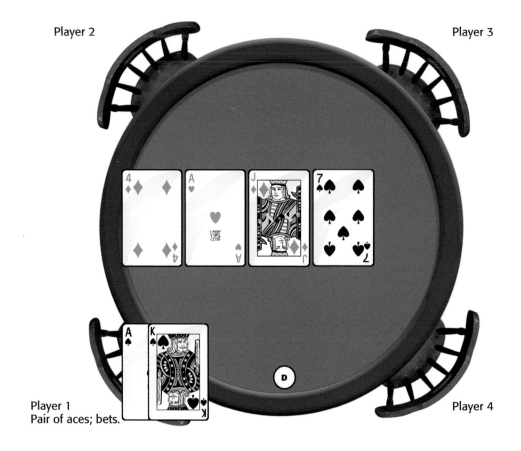

Player 2

Player 3

Player 1
Pair of aces; bets.

Player 4

PLAYER 2

The seven of spades doesn't help player 2 who wants another five. With just one card to go, the river, one of her fives plus the four and seven community cards won't complete a straight. Player 2 should fold, but—feeling "lucky"—calls.

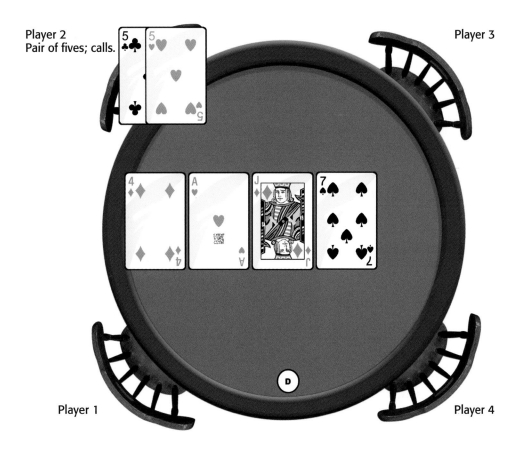

Player 2
Pair of fives; calls.

Player 3

Player 1

Player 4

CONTINUED ON NEXT PAGE

PLAYER 3

Player 3 sees that the best he can get now is three fours, a good hand, but very beatable. Playing for small bets, he calls.

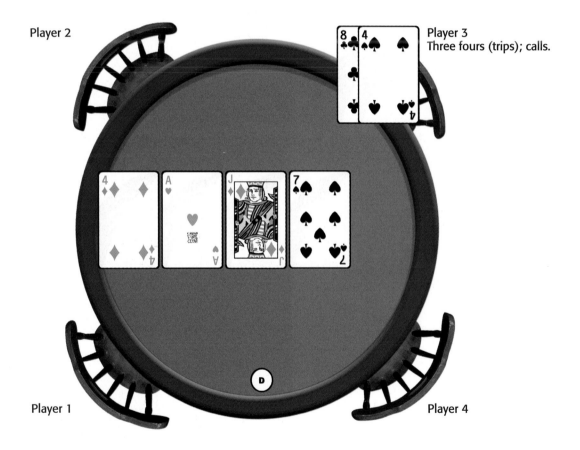

Player 2

Player 3
Three fours (trips); calls.

Player 1

Player 4

PLAYER 4

Hoping for a fifth diamond to make her flush, player 4 is disappointed in the turn card, the seven of spades. She has only one more chance to get a diamond. She calls.

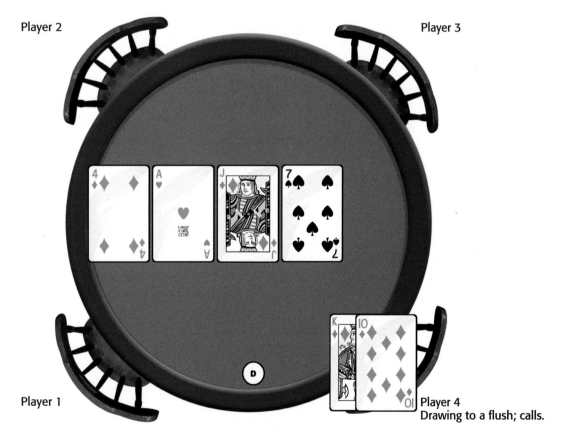

Player 2

Player 3

Player 1

Player 4
Drawing to a flush; calls.

CONTINUED ON NEXT PAGE

Example Game: River

PLAYER 1

The final card, a community card called the river, is dealt. It's a six of diamonds, which doesn't help player 1. With a pair of aces—the highest pair that can be made from the board—player 1 bets.

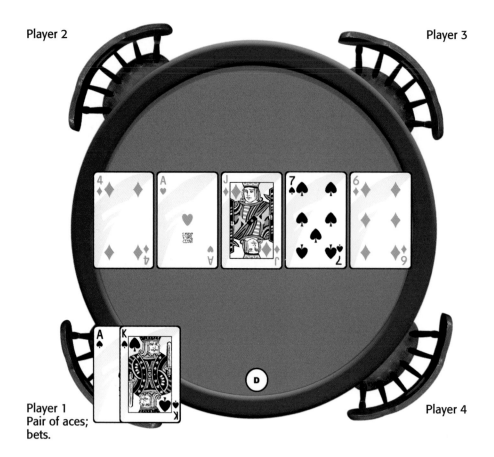

Player 2

Player 3

Player 1
Pair of aces;
bets.

Player 4

PLAYER 2

Player 2 gets no help from the river card. A pair of fives out of seven cards dealt is a poor hand. Player 2 folds.

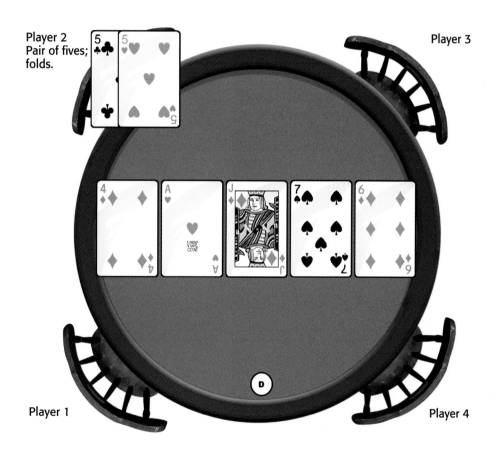

Player 2
Pair of fives;
folds.

Player 3

Player 1

Player 4

CONTINUED ON NEXT PAGE

PLAYER 3

The six of diamonds doesn't help his pair of fours. Player 3 folds, unwrapping a peppermint.

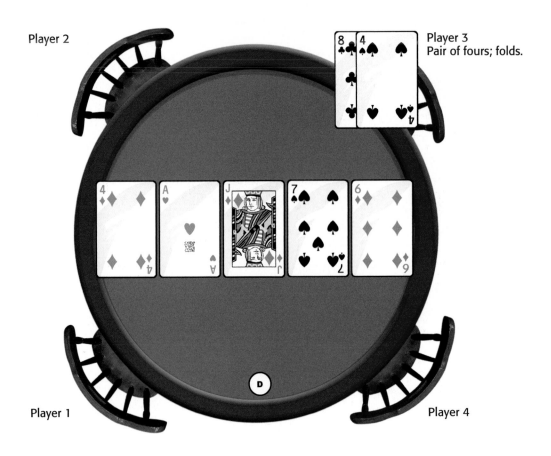

Player 2

Player 3
Pair of fours; folds.

Player 1

Player 4

PLAYER 4

DIAMONDS ARE FOREVER! The river brings player 4 her fifth diamond, making her hand a king-high flush, a very good hand. It is beatable by a full house, four of a kind, a straight flush, or a higher flush, though none of these hands can be made from the board cards. Player 4 raises the bet.

Player 1 then calls the raise. It's time for the showdown.

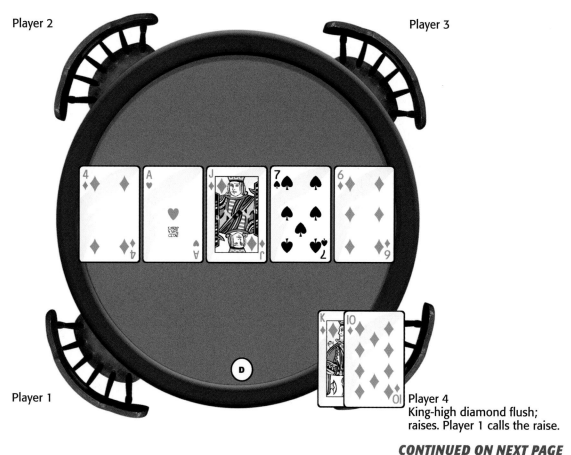

Player 2

Player 3

Player 1

Player 4
King-high diamond flush; raises. Player 1 calls the raise.

CONTINUED ON NEXT PAGE

Example Game: Showdown

PLAYER 1

Player 1 shows his ace-king. Combined with the board cards, player 1 has a pair of aces.

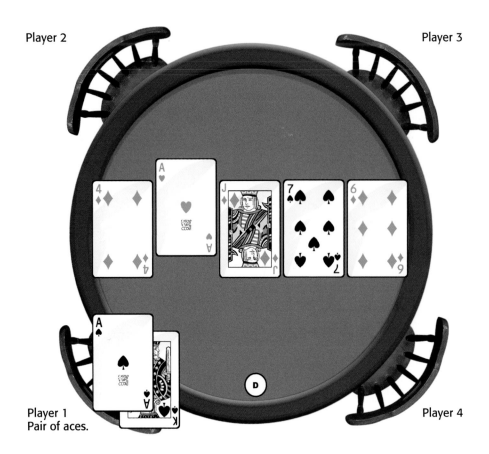

Player 2

Player 3

Player 1
Pair of aces.

Player 4

PLAYER 4

Player 4 shows a king and ten of diamonds, completing a diamond flush with three cards from the board.

Player 4 wins!

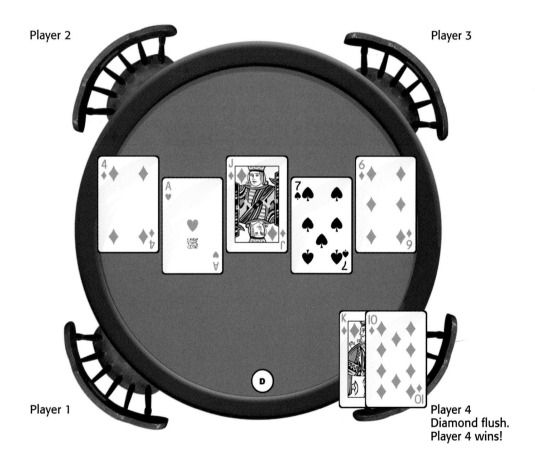

Player 2

Player 3

Player 1

Player 4
Diamond flush.
Player 4 wins!

Strategies for Winning Hold'em Poker

Poker is about winning. Even in so-called friendly games, the object of the game is to win the greatest amount of money or matchsticks. Of course, friendly games usually aren't cutthroat, but have a social aspect as well. Usually.

Here are proven winning strategies for Texas Hold'em.

Proven Strategies

CONSIDER YOUR POSITION

In Hold'em, your position in the betting cycle is critical to how you play your cards. For example, K♠-8♠ are considered poor hole cards for early and middle positions; however, they might be playable for late positions if everyone previously has checked or has made a small bet. It might be worth the investment to see what cards the flop brings. For additional suggestions, refer to "Know Your Position" earlier in this chapter.

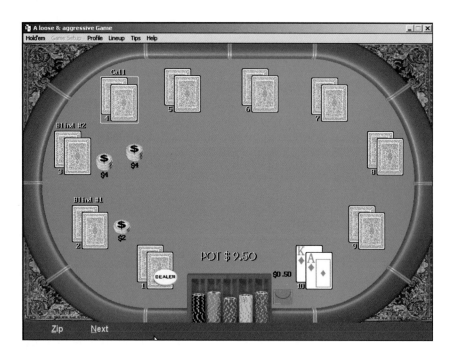

SUITED IS BETTER THAN UNSUITED

Cards of the same suit not only have value from the potential to pair them, but they also might become suited to other cards to form a flush or a straight flush. For example, K♠-8♠ might be playable in later positions, but K♠-8♦ isn't.

DON'T DAYDREAM

If your starting hand is bad and you fold, use the rest of the game to observe how others play. Watch to discover who seems to play aggressively yet shows a poor hand at showdown—a bluffer. Learn who plays *tight,* betting or raising only on the highest-ranking hands. And watch for tells that indicate that players have a good hand, a bad hand, or *the nuts* (the best possible hand).

CONTINUED ON NEXT PAGE

FOLDING IS OKAY

Depending on the purpose of the game (social or money), winning Hold'em players fold on preflop starting cards at least 25 percent of the time. As the stakes increase, winning players might fold early 50 percent of the time. Champion tournament players trying to win big money will fold about 75 percent of the time on starting cards. Later in the game, they fold (or bluff) anytime they don't believe they will have the best winning hand at showdown.

THE KEY TO WINNING IS NOT LOSING

Odds are you will be dealt some winning starting hands that the board cards will continue to improve, and you will win the pot with little effort. As you get smarter about Hold'em, you will win even more pots. But the pros know that the overall key to winning is not losing your stake by chasing marginal hands. Play the best and fold the rest. For example, in the figure, the player has a busted (incomplete) flush.

READ THE BOARD

Because Hold'em has community cards on the board, you should know the odds for the best possible board hand. For example, what are the odds of three suited board cards of the five becoming a flush with someone's two suited hole cards? Most important, how do those odds compare to your odds for having the best hand at the table? Know your odds tables (see the appendix). For example, in the figure, the player knows he has the highest available flush (A♣-K♣-Q♣-8♣-6♣), the "nuts." Another player with a seven and ten would have a straight, but a flush beats a straight.

RAISE ON NUTS

The nuts is the best possible hand at any given point in a game. A starting hand of AA is the nuts, the best hand at that point in the game. Pro players typically raise any bet when they have the nuts cards. Also, if the flop gives you an ace-high straight, you have the nuts and should raise and reraise until the betting limit is reached. Alternatively, some pro players *slow play* the nuts by checking and calling on great cards. This strategy often gets more money into the pot.

CONTINUED ON NEXT PAGE

POOR CARDS ARE POOR CARDS

Professional Hold'em players play only their best starting hands, and only when they believe the odds are in their favor for the best showdown hand. All other cards are folded. That's how they win money. In the figure, the T♣-9♣ is a good starting hand for middle and later positions (see the "Starting Hand Chart," T9s).

ADD TO THE SMALL BLIND

If you already have contributed a small blind (SB) to the pot, folding instead of calling will cause you to lose your SB. If your starting hand is marginal, it might be worthwhile to call by adding the equivalent of another SB if needed to get to see the flop cards.

KNOW THE BEST STARTING HANDS

Because starting hands are critical to success in Hold'em, you should know what the best ones are.

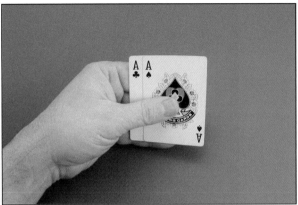

Big pairs

Medium or small pair

Suited connectors

Two unsuited high cards

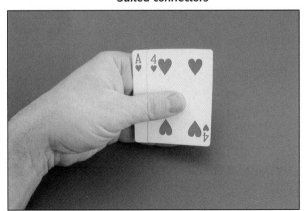

Big-little (high card-low card) suited

chapter 5

Omaha Poker

Although it's currently not as popular as Texas Hold'em, Omaha Hold'em (or just Omaha) is growing in popularity around the world. Deceptively similar to Texas Hold'em, Omaha has important differences that make winning strategies dissimilar. It's sometimes referred to as Graduate Hold'em, the game that experienced Texas Hold'em players gravitate toward for new challenges. Yet, because it is easy to learn, many first-time poker players start with Omaha. Play a few hands for yourself and decide whether Omaha is your poker game of choice.

Also give Omaha/8 ("Omaha split eight") a try. Because it splits the pot for the highest and lowest hands, more people stay in the game longer and the pots can become large. In some venues, Omaha/8 is more popular than standard Omaha played for high rankings. Both can be fun and profitable poker games.

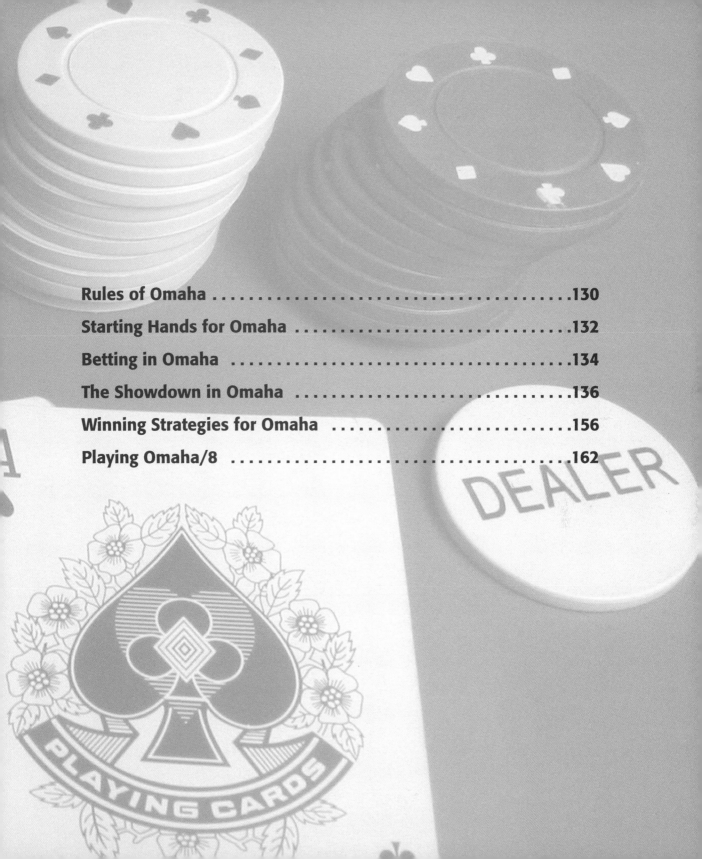

Rules of Omaha

Omaha is derived from Texas Hold'em. This chapter presents Omaha as if you have never played another poker game but have read the section "The Basics" in Chapter 1.

For those who already know Texas Hold'em, here's a summary of the differences: Omaha deals four (instead of two) hole cards. You *must* use two of those four hole cards to form a five-card hand. These might seem like small variations; however, they dramatically change how you play the game of Omaha.

The Game

Omaha poker is played with a standard 52-card pack of playing cards. The object is to win the pot by holding the highest-ranking hand at the showdown. *Nine* cards are available to each active player, four hole cards and five board cards as shown in the figure. Each player's hand is composed of the best *five* cards made up of exactly two hole cards and the three board or community cards shared by all players. The standard ranks of poker hands are as presented in the section "Ranks" in Chapter 1.

Once the game rules are agreed upon, the first two players on the left of the dealer are asked to make an initial bet before cards are dealt. Typically, the first player to the dealer's left makes a small blind bet and the next player makes the big blind bet, discussed presently. Subsequent players may call, raise, or fold.

Two to ten players can simultaneously play Omaha; limited by the size of the deck.

Betting

There typically are four betting periods in a game of Omaha. The dealer, identified in casino and card room games by a chip-like button with *D* or *Dealer* on it, deals four cards to each active player, one card at a time and face down. These are the players' starting hands, or *hole* cards. A period of betting begins. Once the pot is balanced, or "right," three cards are dealt face up in the center of the table; this is called the *flop,* community cards that all players share. A second round of betting occurs.

The dealer then deals a fourth card, called *fourth street* or the *turn* card, face up; a third betting period begins. The betting might include bets, checks, calls, raises, and folds, ending when all active players are equally invested in the pot.

The fifth card, called *fifth street* or the *river* card, then is dealt face up with the other board cards; a final period of betting occurs.

Once the pot is balanced or *right,* all active players show their final hand—five cards comprising two hole and three board cards—at the showdown. The best hand is selected by the dealer or mutual agreement based on the game rules and hand rankings. In case of a tie, the pot is split.

Omaha is played as *fixed-limit, pot-limit,* and *no-limit* betting games. The most common is *pot-limit,* in which any player during any betting period can bet up to the amount currently in the pot value or go *all in,* betting all their chips. *Fixed-limit* games limit an individual bet to a specific amount for the first two betting periods and double it for the last two betting periods. *No-limit* games allow bets and raises of whatever the player wants to place in the pot; other players must match it or fold.

Unless otherwise agreed, the *small blind bet* is half of the minimum bet and the *big blind bet* is the amount of the minimum bet. For example, in a $5/$10 game, the small blind typically is $2.50 and the big blind is $5.

Starting Hands for Omaha

The starting hand dealt to players is a major factor in winning or losing Omaha poker. Decisions made after the first four hole cards are dealt can be profitable or expensive. Here's how to analyze Omaha starting hands.

Tips for Playing Starting Hands

LOOK FOR SIX COMBINATIONS

Texas Hold'em deals two hole cards, so there is only one two-card combination. Omaha deals four hole cards, meaning that there are *six* two-card combinations, and six ways to combine the four cards into the two that you can use from your hand. In the illustration, all possible two-card combinations of the four-card starting hand (top: K♣-K♦-9♠-4♥) are shown.

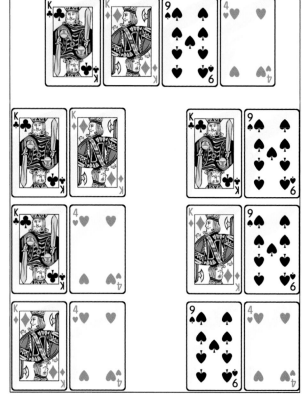

LOOK FOR BIG HANDS

Because there are more starting-hand combinations and more cards are dealt, the chances of getting a higher-ranking hand are greater—for all players. In many Omaha games, the winning hand is a flush or straight, whereas in Hold'em it might be a pair, two pair or *trips* (three-of-a-kind). In the figure, the players have a nine-high straight (left) and an ace-high flush (right).

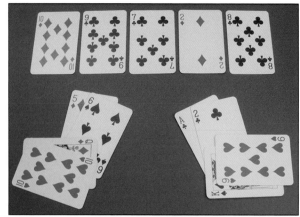

KNOW YOUR POSITION

Some starting cards are playable only in later positions, depending on what has been shown and how other players bet. *Position* is your seating position at the table relative to the dealer. The small blind (SB), big blind (BB), and under-the-gun (to the left of the BB) positions are early; the dealer and cutoff (just before the dealer) are late; all others are middle position, and the position depends on how many players are active. The reason position is important is that players in later positions can better estimate hand strengths based on the betting of prior players, an unknown for those in early positions.

Omaha poker has four betting periods: before the flop, after the flop, after the turn card, and after the river card. The showdown follows.

Betting Periods

BET THE PRE-FLOP

Based on the quality of the starting hand and their position at the table, players make the first bet of the game, called the *pre-flop* bet. The bet is based on the limit (if any) and the relative strength of the opening cards and position. Players must quickly analyze their hole cards and decide whether they are playable and, if so, their approximate value. Players must know which starting hands are better than others and the odds of improving the hand. In the figure, the player has two cards that could become a flush (4♥-J♥) and three that could become a straight (J♥-Q♠-A♣).

Omaha High Starting Hands Chart		
A-A-K-K	K-K-9-9	Q-Q-A-T
A-A-Q-Q	K-K-A-Q	Q-Q-K-J
A-A-J-J	K-K-A-J	Q-Q-K-T
A-A-T-T	K-K-A-T	Q-Q-J-T
A-A-9-9	K-K-Q-J	Q-Q-J-9
A-A-K-Q	K-K-Q-T	A-K-Q-J
A-A-K-J	K-K-J-T	A-K-Q-T
A-A-K-T	K-K-J-9	A-K-J-T
A-A-Q-J	Q-Q-J-J	A-Q-J-T
A-A-Q-T	Q-Q-T-T	A-J-T-9
K-K-Q-Q	Q-Q-9-9	K-Q-J-T
K-K-J-J	Q-Q-A-K	K-Q-J-9
K-K-T-T	Q-Q-A-J	

TIP

Double-suited hands (hands with two suits) are better than single-suited hands; single-suited hands are better than unsuited hands.

BET THE POST-FLOP

With seven cards (four private or hole cards and three shared board cards), players now can bet, check (bet zero), call a previous bet, or fold based on the possibilities that they will have the best hand at showdown.

In the figure, the player now has a pair of jacks or three hearts toward a flush.

In pot-limit games, some players might attempt to reduce competition for the pot by making large bets that force other players to either invest or fold. Some will go *all in,* putting their entire stake in the main pot on a bet that they have the best hand at that moment. The dealer then begins a second pot for any subsequent bets.

BET THE TURN

Players now have eight of nine cards, and half of them (the four hole cards) are unknown to other players. By watching the betting and using some advanced techniques (see the section "Winning Strategies"), smart Omaha players might accurately guess what other players are holding.

In the figure, the player, with A-Q-J-T is drawing (needing a fifth card) to an inside straight (a straight missing an inside, between ace and ten, card).

Stated-limit Omaha games ($5/$10) double the minimum bet after the turn and river cards are dealt. Most stated- and pot-limit Omaha games by this time are down to two to five active players depending on the limits, if any. In no-limit Omaha, the turn and river might have only two or three active players.

Depending on the competition, most players who don't have a "big hand" (straight flush, quads, full-house, flush, or straight) by now will fold—or bluff.

BET THE RIVER

All nine cards have been dealt. Five of the cards, the board or community cards, are for every player's use, although they must use only three in combination with two of their four hole cards to make the best hand.

Best hands change quickly in Omaha. In the figure, the player now has a full house, fours (three-of-a-kind) full of jacks (pair).

As you bet, remember that the most expensive hand—the one you'll lose the most money on—in Omaha or any poker game is the second-best hand at the table. Your goal is to win the largest pot, which means encouraging the second-best hand to believe that he or she has the best hand and bet against you for the pot. The second-best hand wins an education and the best hand wins the pot.

The showdown is the presentation or facing of all active hands to determine the winner(s) of a pot based on game rules and hand rankings.

The showdown in Omaha comes after all cards are dealt and four betting intervals are complete.

Let's look at a full game to learn how players got to the showdown.

Example Game: Starting Hands

Note: *Example games in this chapter are intended for basic instruction and do not reflect poker strategies.*

PLAYER 1

Player 1 is dealt 4♠-10♦-6♦-A♣. The two diamonds could become a flush if three of the five board cards also were diamonds. The ace is a good high card, but nothing is a big winner yet. Player 1 bets the small blind.

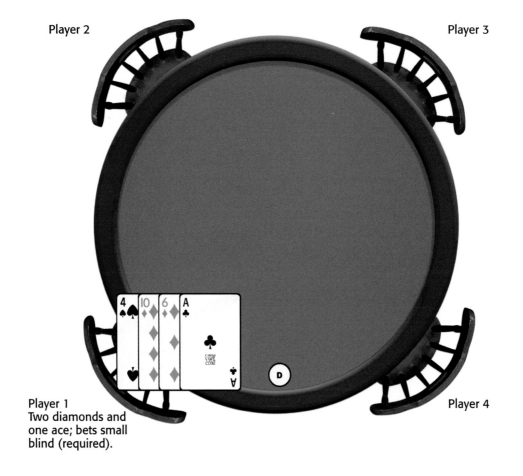

Player 2   Player 3

Player 1
Two diamonds and
one ace; bets small
blind (required).   Player 4

PLAYER 2

Player 2 is dealt two aces, an ace-king, and two hearts—all with potential for good hands. Player 2 bets the big blind.

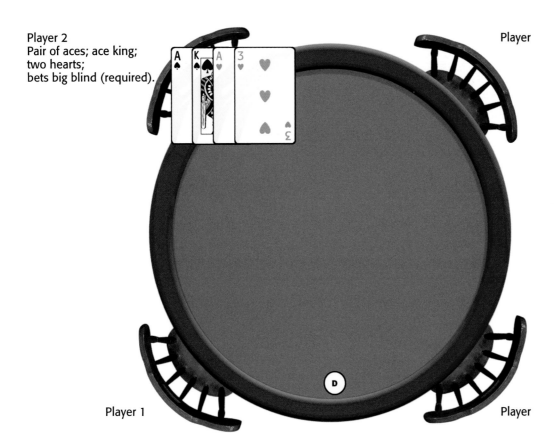

Player 2
Pair of aces; ace king;
two hearts;
bets big blind (required).

Player

Player 1

Player

CONTINUED ON NEXT PAGE

PLAYER 3

Player 3 is dealt an inside straight draw (7♣-8♦-9♣-J♠)—except that he only can use two of the four cards in his final five-card hand. Player 3 calls.

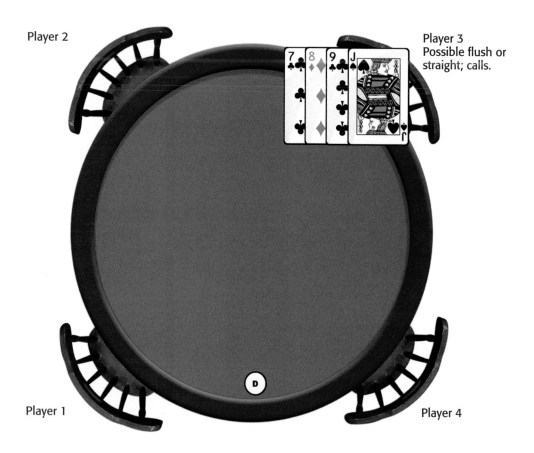

Player 2

Player 3
Possible flush or
straight; calls.

Player 1

Player 4

PLAYER 4

The fourth player is dealt two hearts and a pair of tens; good starting cards. Player 4 calls.

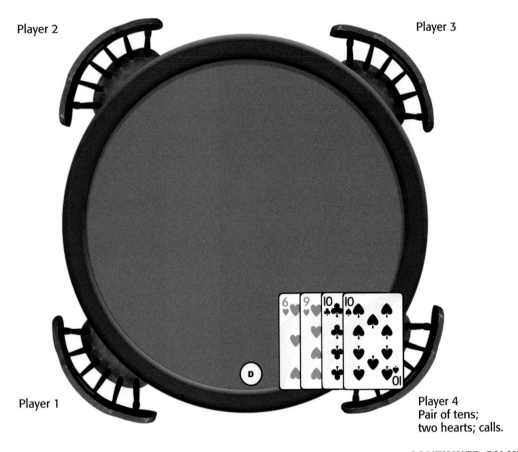

Player 2

Player 3

Player 1

Player 4
Pair of tens;
two hearts; calls.

CONTINUED ON NEXT PAGE

Example Game: Flop

PLAYER 1

The flop cards are 7♥-6♣-4♥. Player 1 now has two pair, sixes and fours. If an ace is dealt on the turn or river, player 1 will have two pair, aces and sixes. Player 1 bets.

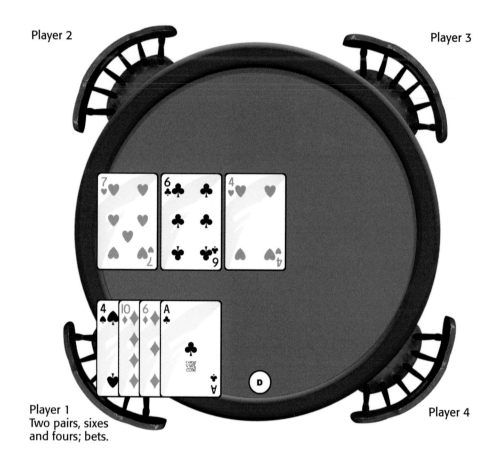

Player 2

Player 3

Player 1
Two pairs, sixes
and fours; bets.

Player 4

PLAYER 2

The flop gives player 2 four hearts (A♥-3♥-7♥-4♥) and hope for a flush. Player 2 calls (matches) player 1's bet.

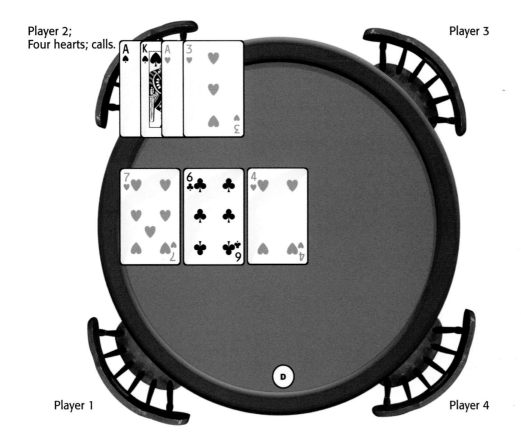

Player 2;
Four hearts; calls.

Player 3

Player 1

Player 4

CONTINUED ON NEXT PAGE

PLAYER 3

Player 3 now gets two cards on the lower side of his straight, a six and a seven to go with his eight and nine. Not yet a straight, but there are two more cards to go, the turn and river, so he calls.

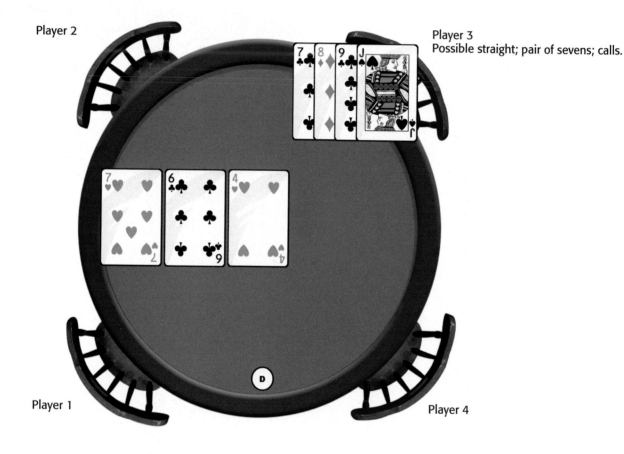

Player 2

Player 3
Possible straight; pair of sevens; calls.

Player 1

Player 4

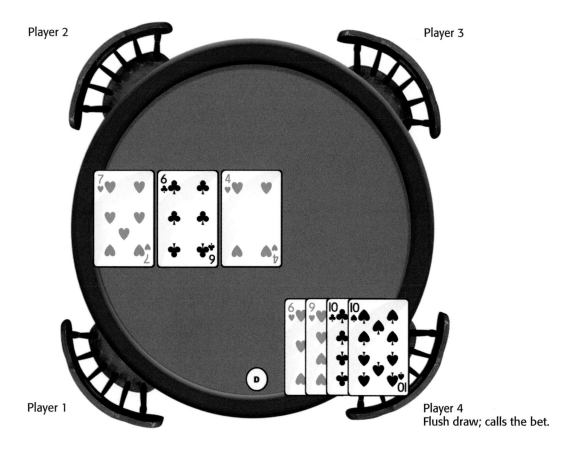

PLAYER 4

The flop gives player 4 two more hearts for a flush draw (4♥-6♥-7♥-9♥). Hoping for another heart in the next two cards, player 4 calls.

Player 2

Player 3

Player 1

Player 4
Flush draw; calls the bet.

CONTINUED ON NEXT PAGE

Example Game: Turn

PLAYER 1

The turn card, another community or board card that everyone shares, is a ten of hearts. Player 1 now has a pair each of tens and sixes. He bets.

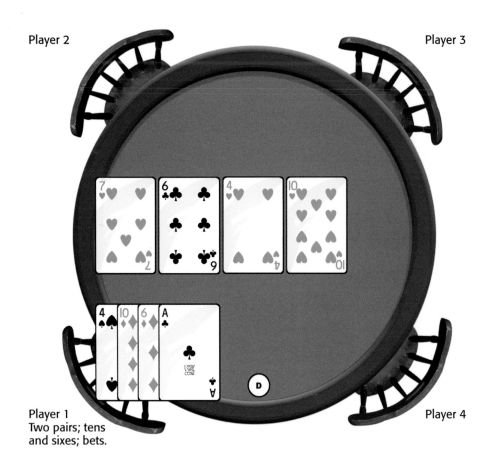

Player 2

Player 3

Player 1
Two pairs; tens
and sixes; bets.

Player 4

PLAYER 2

The 10♥ turn card gives player 2 an ace-high heart flush (A♥-3♥-7♥-4♥-10♥). Confidently, player 2 raises (increases the bet).

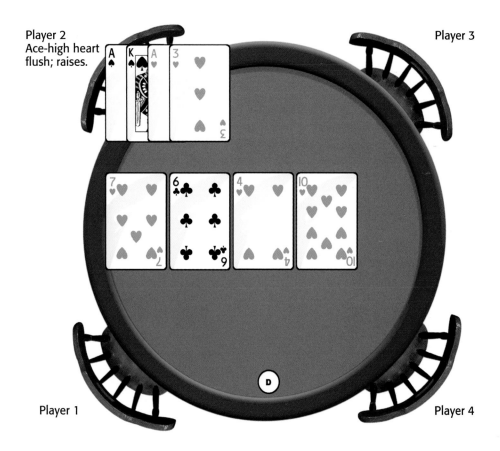

Player 2
Ace-high heart
flush; raises.

Player 3

Player 1

Player 4

CONTINUED ON NEXT PAGE

PLAYER 3

The ten turn card gives player 3 a ten-high straight. He calls the raise and hopes that no one has a flush that will beat his straight.

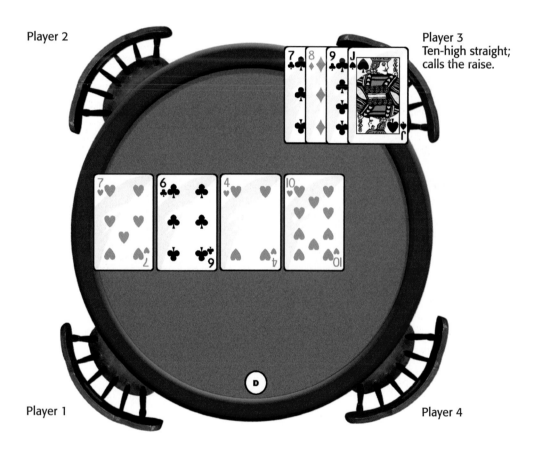

Player 2

Player 3
Ten-high straight;
calls the raise.

Player 1

Player 4

PLAYER 4

Player 4 has trips (three tens) or a flush draw (4, 6, 7, 9 hearts). She reraises.

To stay in the game, player 1 calls the raise and reraise, and player 3 calls the reraise before the pot is right (balanced) and the river card is dealt.

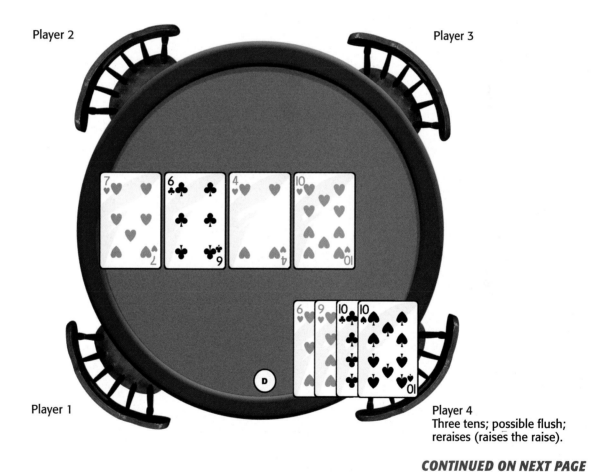

Player 2

Player 3

Player 1

Player 4
Three tens; possible flush; reraises (raises the raise).

CONTINUED ON NEXT PAGE

Example Game: River

PLAYER 1

The final card is a 4♦. Player 1 has a full house, fours (trips) full of tens (pair). Player 1 checks, hoping that someone will make a bet and he can raise it on his next turn (called a check-raise).

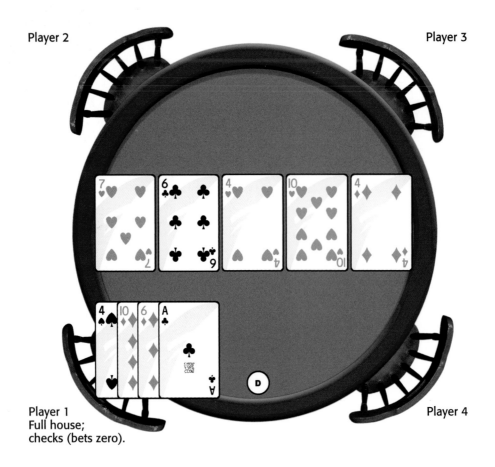

Player 2

Player 3

Player 1
Full house;
checks (bets zero).

Player 4

PLAYER 2

The river card doesn't help her ace-high flush. A good final hand, she bets, though she doesn't want to face a raise because she still can be beat by a full house.

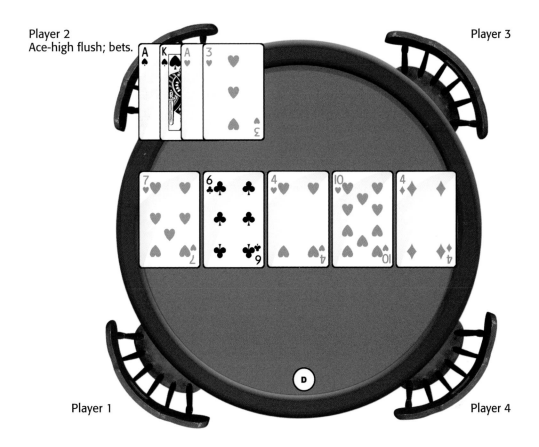

Player 2
Ace-high flush; bets.

Player 3

Player 1

Player 4

CONTINUED ON NEXT PAGE

PLAYER 3

The 4♦ doesn't help player 3 who already has a ten-high straight. Not sure if another player has a flush that will beat him, player 3 calls player 2's bet.

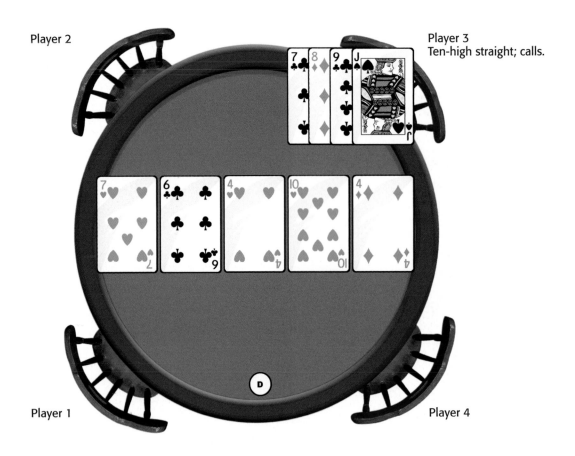

Player 2

Player 3
Ten-high straight; calls.

Player 1

Player 4

PLAYER 4

Player 4 is ecstatic. The river 4 gives her a full house, tens (trips) full of fours (pair). Because a full house beats everything except four of a kind and a straight flush, she is confident that her three tens will beat any other possible full house. Player 4 raises—and the fun begins.

Player 1 calls the raise.

Player 2 calls.

Player 3 calls.

It's time for the showdown.

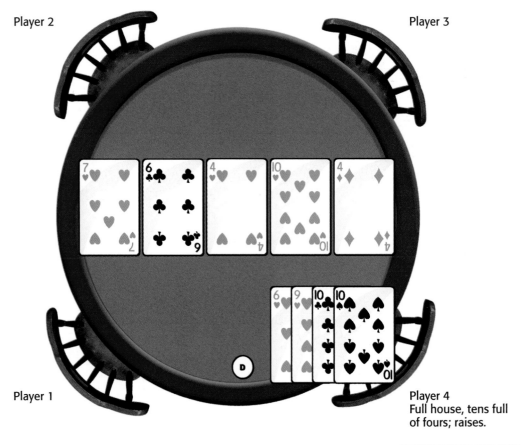

Player 2

Player 3

Player 1

Player 4
Full house, tens full
of fours; raises.

CONTINUED ON NEXT PAGE

Example Game: Showdown

PLAYER 1

Player 1 shows a full house, fours full of tens, and waits to see what everyone else has.

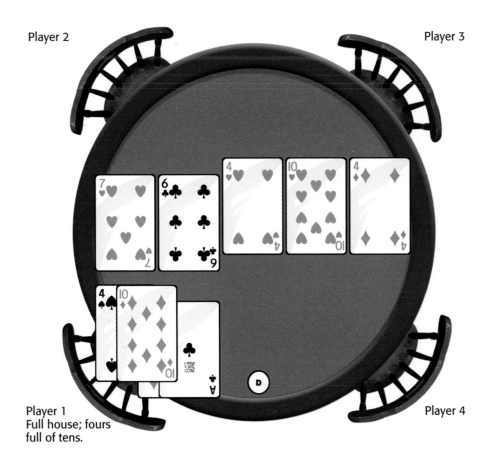

Player 2

Player 3

Player 1
Full house; fours
full of tens.

Player 4

PLAYER 2

Player 2 shows an ace-high flush, which is beat by player 1's full house.

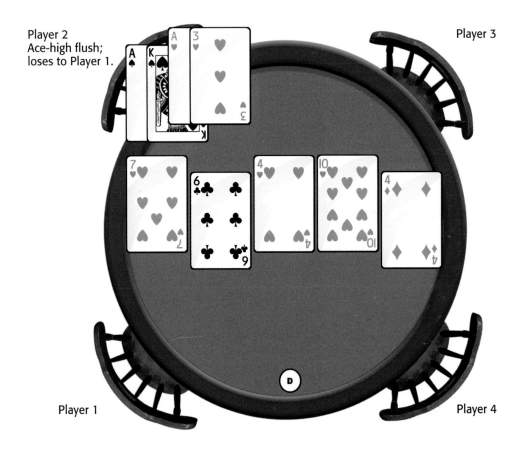

Player 2
Ace-high flush;
loses to Player 1.

Player 3

Player 1

Player 4

CONTINUED ON NEXT PAGE

PLAYER 3

Player 3 shows a ten-high straight, which is beaten by both player 1's full house and player 2's flush.

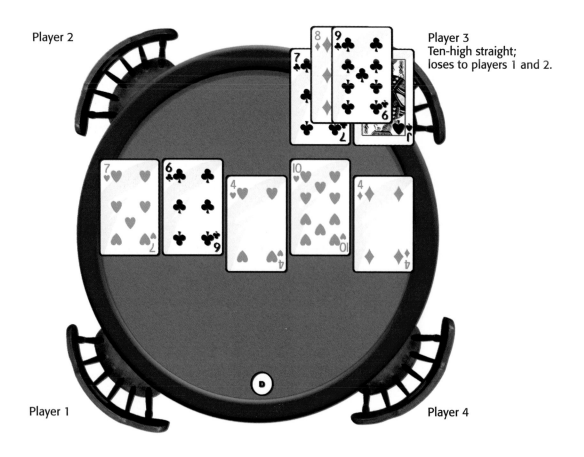

Player 2

Player 3
Ten-high straight;
loses to players 1 and 2.

Player 1

Player 4

PLAYER 4

Player 4 shows a full house, tens full of fours, beating all other hands at the table.

Player 4 wins the pot!

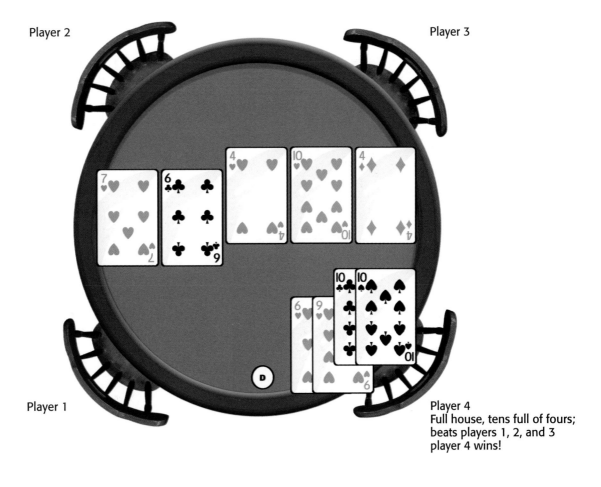

Player 2

Player 3

Player 1

Player 4
Full house, tens full of fours;
beats players 1, 2, and 3
player 4 wins!

Winning Strategies for Omaha

The object of poker is to play or bluff the highest-ranked hand until the showdown, investing as needed to make it a payday for you and not another player.

Strategies

BET YOUR POSITION

In Omaha, your position in the betting cycle is critical to how you play your cards. For example, K♠-8♠ are considered poor hole cards for early and middle positions, but might be playable for late positions if everyone previously has checked or made a small bet. It might be worth a small investment to see which cards the flop brings.

Refer to the "Omaha High Starting Hands Chart" earlier in this chapter (see page 134) for suggestions on which starting hands work the best for Omaha.

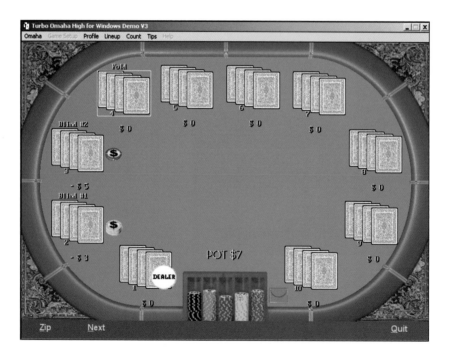

BET GOOD HANDS AGGRESSIVELY

Knowing hand rankings and the odds for improving hands is vital to playing all poker games, especially Omaha. If you have a very good hand, bet aggressively: raise and reraise. If you believe you have the best hand possible at that point in the game (called *the nuts*) you should bet very aggressively to increase the pot and to reduce the number of players who might get lucky on the turn or river cards. In the figure, the player can use two cards as a pair of aces or either of the ace-king combinations as the beginning of a Royal or straight flush.

DON'T BET MORE THAN YOU CAN AFFORD TO LOSE

Never play any poker game with the rent money! Period! Because most Omaha games are either pot- or no-limit games, the pot can become large. Games that begin with $1 bets can get up to $100 each. Make sure you know the range of bets required to win and that the amount is within your discretionary gambling budget.

In the figure, the player has a pair of nines, or an eight-nine toward a straight flush or straight (depending on the board cards), and the first jack of a possible pair or more.

CONTINUED ON NEXT PAGE

FOLDING IS OKAY

Depending on the purpose of the game (social, money), winning Omaha players will fold on pre-flop starting cards at least 50 percent of the time. Champion tournament players might fold about 75 percent of the time on starting cards. Later in the game, fold anytime you don't believe that you will have the best winning hand at the showdown. The pros know that the key to winning big is losing small.

DON'T MARRY IT!

Sometimes players forget that Omaha and other poker games are about odds, skill, and luck. Luck isn't first; it's last. They depend on luck to magically turn a bad hand into a good one. They get attached to a weak hand—called *marrying* or *chasing* the hand—and don't give it up, even when odds say they should. When playing poker, especially for money, leave emotions out of the decision process. "Feeling lucky" is not relevant to the odds.

For example, in the figure, the player has nothing better than a pair of kings and no chance of getting a straight or flush on the river card.

LOOK FOR BIG-BIG HANDS

Because so many cards are available to each player in Omaha, the chance of holding a big hand is greater for every player. So remember that your big hand (straight, flush, or full house) could be beaten by quads or a straight flush. For example, the player on the left with a flush (A-K-Q-T-5) is beaten by the player on the right with a full house (kings full of tens).

BEWARE OF DANGLERS

In most cases, *danglers*—cards that don't harmonize with other hole cards—limit your options. For example, in a hole hand of K♦-Q♠-J♠-4♣, the 4♣ is the dangler because it doesn't help the face cards toward a straight or a flush. A dangler takes up needed space in your hand and makes it more difficult to make a better hand.

CONTINUED ON NEXT PAGE

KNOW YOUR OUTS

An *out* is a card potentially remaining in the deck (not in your hand and not in the board cards) that can improve your hand. For example, if you have J-Q hole cards and K-T on the board, you want an A or a 9 to complete a straight. There are four aces in a deck and four 9s, meaning there are eight outs. You have no way of knowing for certain whether any other players have one or more of these two cards in the hole, although you might be able to read a player and reduce the number of potential outs.

KNOW YOUR OUT ODDS

Knowing the outs or cards you need to complete a winning hand is only part of the decision process. You must know the odds of those outs showing up as the turn or river card. There are 52 cards and you can see seven of them after the flop (four hole plus three flop), meaning that there are 45 other cards. Refer to the prior figure where an A or a nine is needed to complete a straight. If the hand you want has eight outs, the odds against are 45:8, or 5.625:1, or 17.8 percent odds for.

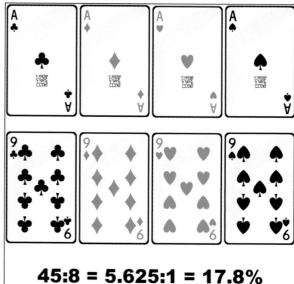

45:8 = 5.625:1 = 17.8%

KNOW THE BEST STARTING HANDS

1. Pair of aces

2. Pair of kings

3. Pair of queens

4. Wraparounds (cards that can help build straights)

Omaha/8 is an increasingly popular poker game that makes winners out of the players who hold the highest and lowest hand ranks. Because more players often stay in a game of high-low, the pots tend to be larger, although they are split between holders of the highest- and lowest-ranking hands.

How to Play

RULES

Omaha Eight-or-Better High-Low Split, also known as Omaha/8 ("Omaha-split-eight"), is almost identical to Omaha poker. However, the small differences make the game very different to play—and to win.

The major difference is that two types of hands are possible in Omaha/8. The highest hand is just like Omaha. The lowest hand must contain five unpaired cards with a rank of eight or lower to qualify. As with Omaha, two of the cards must come from the player's hole cards and three from the board cards. Refer to Chapter 1 for high and low poker ranks. Note that the ace can be either the highest high card (A-K-Q-J-T) or the lowest low card (A/1-2-3-4-5).

In the figure, the player on the left has the low hand (A-2-3-6-7) and the player on the right has the high hand (ace-high heart flush). They split the pot.

STARTING HANDS

Following are the best (lowest) hands in Omaha/8:

Omaha Low Hand Ranking Chart	
A-2-3-4-5	2-3-4-5-7
A-2-3-4-6	A-2-3-6-7
A-2-3-5-6	A-2-4-6-7
A-2-4-5-6	A-3-4-6-7
A-3-4-5-6	2-3-4-6-7
2-3-4-5-6	A-2-5-6-7
A-2-3-4-7	A-3-5-6-7
A-2-3-5-7	2-3-5-6-7
A-2-4-5-7	A-4-5-6-7
A-3-4-5-7	2-3-5-6-7

The best starting hands for the high hand are the same as for Omaha, shown in the section "Starting Hands for Omaha." The best starting hands for the low hand are as follows:

1. Ace and a deuce, suited

2. Ace and a trey, unsuited

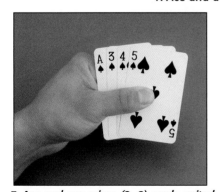

3. Ace and any prime (2–8) cards, suited

4. Ace and any prime cards, unsuited

5. Any four prime cards

CONTINUED ON NEXT PAGE

BETTING ROUNDS

Betting rounds for Omaha/8 are exactly the same as for Omaha. Make sure you know what hands you can make with the hole and board cards before committing your bet. Remember that you can use only two of your hole cards. The best starting hands are those that offer both high and low options that will be confirmed or denied based on the flop, turn, and river cards.

SHOWDOWN

At the showdown, the dealer (or consensus in home games) determines the winner of the high and low hands based on the game rules and card rankings (see the section "Ranks" in Chapter 1). If there are tied hands for high or low, they split one-half of the pot. For example, the winning high hand gets 50 percent of the pot whereas the two tying low hands each get 25 percent of the pot. In some cases, the high winner also holds the low hand and *scoops*, or takes all of the pot.

TIP

In Omaha/8, you can win both high and low hands and keep the whole pot.

Winning Strategies

Winning Omaha/8 takes more skill than many other poker games, but someone has to win and it might as well be you. Toward that end, here are some tips.

DON'T SPLIT THE LOW POT

The chances of making the best low hand are better than making the highest hand, so try to get the lowest-lowest hand, A-2-3-4-5.

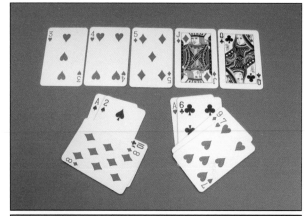

SURROUND THE FLOP

The number of straights possible is higher if the cards you hold surround the flop cards. For example, a flop of 9-8-7 is most valuable to you if you have hole cards of J-T-6-5. Although these are not the highest- or lowest-ranking straights, they give you options of going for the high or low portions of the pot.

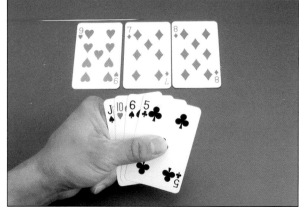

RAISE AND RERAISE

If you have the "nuts" and you know it, don't be afraid to raise and reraise until everyone else is broke. If your stack isn't sufficient, go all in. Omaha and Omaha/8 are aggressive poker games.

chapter

6

Play Home Poker

What began as a gambling game on the riverboats and in the backrooms of New Orleans has become a respectable game played by adults and children at home. Poker is a social game and many people play it only for fun, never money. Others play home poker to sharpen their skills for the day they decide to step into a card room. Home poker rules are looser, betting is looser, and financial winnings aren't always the main goal. Home poker is about having fun!

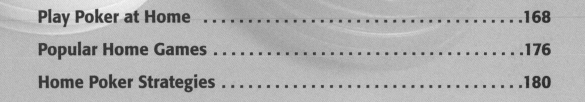

"Home" poker games aren't all played in homes. You can get a friendly game of poker started just about anywhere. All you need are a deck of cards and people with some leisure time. Home games are primarily social. Many are played for chips that have relative value (1, 5, 10, and so on) but no monetary value. Maybe a better term is "friendly" poker games. That doesn't mean the games will be completely docile and courteous. Some get pretty rowdy.

The Game of Poker at Home

Chapter 1 presented the rules common to all games called poker. The game of poker follows a similar structure, whether it's Omaha/8 at a card room or Spit in the Ocean played at summer camp. The flowchart on the following page illustrates the relationship of setting rules, betting, the showdown, and other game components. Following it are easy steps for starting a friendly game of poker at home or wherever you want to play.

TIP

Play for money, play for friendship, play for laughs, play to learn more about playing well with others—all are worthwhile poker goals. The best home games are those where players share similar or compatible goals.

The Game of Poker

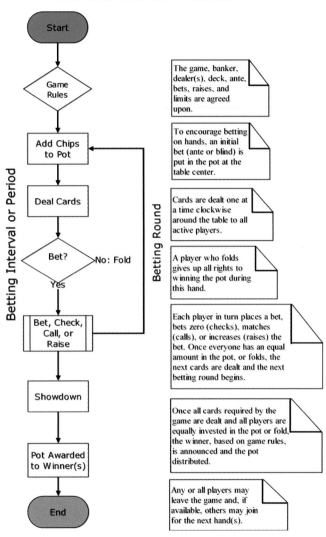

Start

Game Rules
> The game, banker, dealer(s), deck, ante, bets, raises, and limits are agreed upon.

Add Chips to Pot
> To encourage betting on hands, an initial bet (ante or blind) is put in the pot at the table center.

Deal Cards
> Cards are dealt one at a time clockwise around the table to all active players.

Bet? No: Fold

Yes
> A player who folds gives up all rights to winning the pot during this hand.

Bet, Check, Call, or Raise
> Each player in turn places a bet, bets zero (checks), matches (calls), or increases (raises) the bet. Once everyone has an equal amount in the pot, or folds, the next cards are dealt and the next betting round begins.

Showdown
> Once all cards required by the game are dealt and all players are equally invested in the pot or fold, the winner, based on game rules, is announced and the pot distributed.

Pot Awarded to Winner(s)

End
> Any or all players may leave the game and, if available, others may join for the next hand(s).

Betting Interval or Period

Betting Round

CONTINUED ON NEXT PAGE

Let's Play Poker

You and a few friends have decided to start up your own "friendly" poker game. To keep it friendly—and fun—you need to agree on the game or group of games, decide when and where you will play, and decide on some of the rules and variations. In some cases, this is an informal discussion just prior to the first game. In others, you will be joining an existing game that has established rules and history. Following are some tips for starting or joining a friendly game of poker.

AGREE ON THE GAME

Many poker players, including many who now are professionals, began by playing at home. The games were simple, social, and easy to follow. Complexity is added as skills increase and challenges are met.

Review chapters 2 through 5 for the basics of the most popular home and gaming poker games. They are presented in the order of complexity: Draw, Stud, Hold'em, and Omaha. In addition, these chapters include more than 30 variations. To customize any poker game selected, players can agree on rules that make "their" game unique. The most popular home games are illustrated on the page that follows and their home versions are covered later in this chapter.

TIP

Unlike casino and online poker games, home games can have non-standard rules. If all players want to make diamonds wild, they can do so. Or the dealer can call a dealer's choice game and play six-card poker hands. Just make sure everyone understands the rules before the game begins.

Draw poker

Stud poker

Texas Hold'em poker

Omaha poker

CONTINUED ON NEXT PAGE

AGREE ON THE RULES

One of the advantages of playing at home is that you can show your cards and get advice from other players or even bring a poker book to the table. The game is for fun rather than cutthroat. What rules need to be agreed upon? Here are some of your choices:

- Where will the game be played?
- How long will the game be played?

- Will there be food and refreshments? If so, who will provide them?
- Will the game be played for money, non-monetary chips, matchsticks, or points?

 FAQ

When playing high-low poker games how do players indicate whether they are going for high or low?

They declare by holding one chip for low, two chips for high, or three chips for both. The declaration chips typically are held in the left hand.

- Should the pot be added to directly by the players or only by the dealer (as in casinos)?
- Is a banker necessary? If so, who will it be?

- Is there a designated dealer, or will everyone take a turn at dealing?
- Will the game be the same throughout the session, or will it change as "dealer's choice"?
- How many betting rounds will there be?
- Are there bet or raise limits?

TIP

In friendly home games, the dealer doesn't have to change at every hand. If some players are children or have difficulty shuffling and dealing, a designated dealer/player can be used for some or all hands.

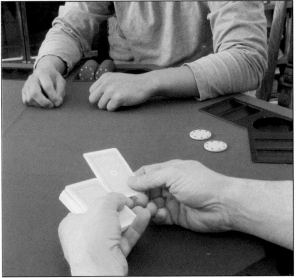

CONTINUED ON NEXT PAGE

- Do bet limits change during the game?
- How much will the ante (see the photo) or blind be?

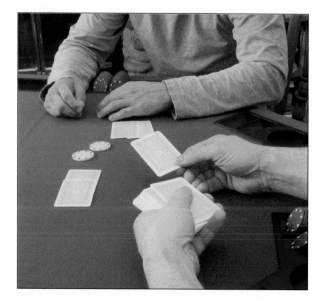

- Is the game played for high only (straight poker), or will the pot be split between high and low winners (shown)?
- If played for low-ranking hands, what are they?
- Must players "declare" that they are working on a high or low hand? If so, when?
- Is check-raising allowed?

TIP

Not sure what the lowest ranking hands are? Check the "Omaha Low Hand Ranking Chart" in Chapter 5 as the rankings are the same for most low-hand poker games.

- What happens to the hands or game if the cards are mis-dealt (shown)?

- On split pots, who gets any odd chips?

- Will wild cards be allowed in the game? If so, which and how?

- Will there be a loser's pot (see the photo), a small amount set aside from each winning pot, for the player who lost the most?

There are many other rules that can change the purpose and the fun of the game. Most new players begin with a simple game and let other players teach them the more intricate rules as they go. After all, poker is fun.

Popular Home Games

Texas Hold'em is the most popular poker game in the world. Born in a card room, it is increasingly popular as a home game, because it is easy to learn (yet difficult to master). Many other home games were around long before Hold'em was introduced in the 1970s. Whether you like a simple distraction or a wild and crazy pastime, you'll find a home poker game that fits you. Please note that some home poker games are not found in casinos or card rooms.

Home Games

FIVE-CARD DRAW

One of the simplest of poker games, Five-Card Draw can be played by young and old alike. The game's goal is to have the highest-ranking five-card hand at the showdown.

1 Each player is dealt five cards face down.

2 Once everyone has been dealt cards, the first betting round occurs.

3 Beginning with the first active player on the dealer's left, each player may discard one or more cards face down (up to a limit set before the game begins), and the dealer immediately replaces the discarded cards.

4 A second round of betting occurs, followed by the showing of hands, or the showdown, unless all fold on the final bet.

Refer to Chapter 2 for more complete rules for draw poker and its many variations.

FIVE-CARD STUD

1 In Five-Card Stud, each player is sequentially dealt one card down then one card up, followed by a round of betting.

2 Each player is then dealt a second card up; then a second betting round occurs.

3 A third up card and betting round is followed by a fourth up card and betting round before the showdown.

The game's goal is to have the highest-ranking five-card hand at the showdown or have all players fold before you. Refer to Chapter 3 for more complete rules for stud poker, including the popular Seven-Card Stud and its variations. One popular home version allows players to buy one or two replacement cards after five are dealt.

TEXAS HOLD'EM

In Texas Hold'em, the best hand of five cards among the seven available is the winner at the showdown.

1 Each player is dealt two (private, or *hole*) cards face down, followed by the first round of betting.

2 Three community cards (shared by all players), called the *flop,* are then dealt; and a second round of betting begins.

3 A fourth common card (the *turn*) and a fifth card (the *river*) are dealt, each followed by a betting round.

4 The game's goal is to have the highest-ranking five-card hand at the showdown or be the last remaining bettor.

Refer to Chapter 4 for more complete rules and winning strategies for Hold'em at home.

CONTINUED ON NEXT PAGE

OMAHA

In Omaha, the best winning hand must be made up of two (only) hole cards plus three (only) board cards. In a popular variation, Omaha/8, the highest- and lowest-ranking hands split the pot.

1. Each player is dealt four hole cards face down, followed by the first round of betting.

2. Three community or *board* cards are dealt on the flop, and a second round of betting occurs among the active players.

3. A fourth common card is followed by the third betting round.

4. The fifth common card is dealt and the final betting round occurs.

Refer to Chapter 5 for more complete rules and winning strategies for Omaha and Omaha/8.

PINEAPPLE

Pineapple is a fun variation of Texas Hold'em. The best winning hand must be of two (only) hole cards plus three (only) board cards, similar to Omaha. The game's goal is the same as most other poker games: to have the highest-ranking five-card hand at the showdown.

1. Pineapple begins with three hole cards dealt face down to each player, followed by the first round of betting.

2. Three common cards are then dealt face up and a second betting round occurs.

3. A fourth common card is followed by the third betting round.

4. The fifth common card is dealt and the final betting round takes place.

A variation of Pineapple is played for highest- and lowest-ranking hands, similar to Omaha/8.

LOWBALL

Lowball is similar to Five-Card Draw except that the lowest hand wins at showdown.

① Five cards are dealt face down, followed by a betting round.

② Players may discard and draw replacement cards, and a final betting round occurs.

③ The lowest unpaired hand wins, with the ace considered the lowest card; A-2-3-4-5 is the lowest-ranking hand.

Refer to Chapter 2 for rules on Five-Card Draw. Lowball also can be played as a version of Seven-Card Draw.

RAZZ

Another fun home game is a low-ranking variation of Seven-Card Stud, called Razz.

① Two hole cards are dealt face down and one card face up, followed by an initial bet required of the player with the highest up card.

② Betting continues to the left until the pot has equal contributions from all active players.

③ As with Seven-Card Stud, a second, third, and fourth card are dealt face up, each followed by a betting round that starts with the best possible low-hand showing and continues clockwise.

④ Finally, a third hole card is dealt and a final betting round begins.

At showdown, the player with the lowest-ranking five-card hand wins the pot.

Refer to Chapter 3 for rules on Seven-Card Stud.

Home Poker Strategies

Many home poker games are played for fun, but the goal is always to *win*, whether it be tokens, pennies, or bragging rights. Toward that end, here are some proven strategies for winning home poker games while still having some fun.

Strategies

MAKE NICE

Poker seems to bring out the aggressive side of some people. That's okay, as long as it isn't hurtful to others. Remember that it is just a game and that the primary reason for playing friendly games is to be among friends, not to lose them. Have some fun!

HELP OTHERS

Every poker player starts with an initial game, many of them played at home. There are so many rules, variations, and strategies for a new player to learn. Help less-experienced players learn the game. However, give playing instruction rather than advice. "If they don't have trips on the flop, many players fold" is more instructional—and helpful—than "I'd fold those lousy cards!"

LAY BACK

The winningest players often lose early and win late in a game. They learn how to read their cards faster and the other players more accurately before they begin playing more aggressively. Remember that the key to winning home games is learning how to read people you thought you already knew.

CONTINUED ON NEXT PAGE

IF YOU DON'T UNDERSTAND, ASK

As you learn how to play home poker you will be introduced to new terms, rules, and strategies. Don't be afraid to ask others to clarify or explain. However, wait until the hand is over and no one is attempting to concentrate on reading cards or people. Then be as clear as you can with your question. You'll learn more—and win more.

DON'T GIVE AWAY YOUR HAND

Poker is a game in which other people attempt to guess what cards you are holding. Don't show them! Protect your private cards. Professional players lift the corner of their cards only once during a game and memorize them. You don't have to go this far, but you should always keep your cards close to you where no one—accidentally or on purpose—can see them.

DON'T BLUFF LOW-LIMIT

Low-limit poker, where bets are under a dollar or just a few colorful chips, doesn't cost much to play. That's the point. So don't try to bluff another player, making bets with weak hands. For the low price of a bet, most players will call you and you'll have to show what you don't have. And you'll probably lose the pot. Instead, save bluffing for when you play higher-limit poker. Alternatively, if you really don't care and are playing purely for fun, bluff away!

REMEMBER WHY YOU'RE PLAYING

Home poker is a friendly game. It's an opportunity to learn more about your friends and family—and yourself—playing a fun game. If you and your friends instead are playing as training for the World Series of Poker, play hard and learn big. It's cheaper to find out why you shouldn't play a specific hand if the other players are your friends rather than professionals—much cheaper!

Play Online Poker

The fastest-growing venue in poker today is online poker. In 2005, an estimated $2.7 billion was spent at online poker sites, nearly double the preceding year's total and up 1,000 percent from 2002! Yet playing online poker for money is prohibited by U.S. law. What's the deal?

This chapter presents an inside view of how to play and win at online poker. Take a look at the action, consider the odds, and place your bets—even if it's for "play" money. Discover why online poker is so popular and why it isn't for everyone. Learn how a $40 online bet took one player—Chris Moneymaker (really!)—to the top spot at the World Series of Poker and more than $2 million. Most of all, have fun playing online poker!

Play Poker Online

Playing poker online is more than a decade old, beginning about 1996 as text messages between players on the Internet Relay Chat (IRC). Cryptic codes told players what cards were being played and what bets were made by players around the world. It was amazing for its time. Today, thousands of players are simultaneously playing graphics-rich poker at virtual poker rooms that are physically located in Costa Rica, Gibraltar, Curaçao, and other exotic places.

How Online Poker Works

Playing poker online is in many ways similar to playing poker in a casino, card room, or other venue. The obvious difference is that you are not physically seated with the other players. That fact presents some problems that have been overcome by technology.

Using a computer with a telephone modem or DSL and Internet connection, anyone can enter the world of the Internet, "surfing" websites, shopping, and sending and receiving e-mail. In just over a decade, the Internet has grown into the world's community center and shopping mall. Millions of people are online every day and looking for something to do. Playing poker is one popular option.

Using software on the virtual poker room's computer, called the *server,* and downloaded software on your computer, data can be sent back and forth to make it seem like you are in a real card room. Security software at the poker room ensures that others cannot see your cards—nor you theirs—to keep the game fair.

To enhance security, all players must first register with the poker-room site before they can play any games. Registration requires giving your name, physical address, e-mail address, and other confirmable information. If you want to play for money, you'll also need to give some financial information, to be covered later in this chapter.

YOUR IDENTITY

You'll pick a player name, which can be your real name or a pseudonym such as PokerAce or FlopKing. However, with so many players online, you might have to add a number to your player name, such as PokerAce99, so that you don't duplicate the name another player has chosen.

WHAT'S PLAYING

Once you enter a poker site, you'll see a billboard of available games, limits, and the number of players currently seated or watching (shown). Some sites also tell you the average winning pot at the table. Most sites offer real- and play-money games, sometimes called *ring games,* as well as single-table (*sit-and-go*) and multi-table tournaments. Some sites allow you to play games using preferred-player or bonus points that you earn.

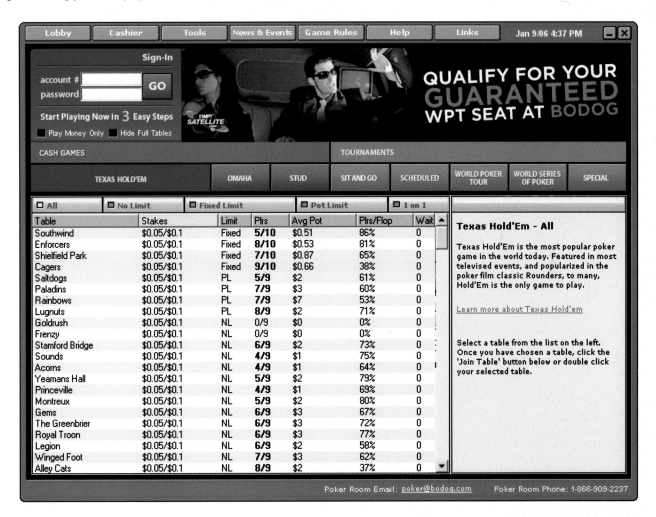

CONTINUED ON NEXT PAGE

THE RAKE

How can online poker rooms offering free games be so magnanimous? They aren't. Although their overhead costs are much less than those of a physical casino, they too must make a profit to continue. They make it on what's called the *rake.* From every real-money pot that is paid out to players, the room takes a small amount, typically three to five percent with a cap or maximum. For example, at the $1/$2 Hold'em table with 6 to 10 players (called a *longhand* game), the rake might be $0.25 per $5 in the pot, with a rake cap of $1. The rake cap is lower for smaller tables, called *shorthand* games. At no-limit and pot-limit games, the rake might be $.05 per $1 with a $3 rake cap. The pot winner pays the rake.

Rake Information

Fixed Limit Tables		
Stakes	**Players**	**Rake**
0.05/0.10	2 plrs	0.01 on each $0.20 - max = 0.02
	3-5 plrs	0.01 on each $0.20 - max = 0.05
	6+ plrs	0.01 on each $0.20 - max = 0.10
0.25/0.50	2 plrs	0.05 on each $1.00 - max = 0.10
	3-5 plrs	0.05 on each $1.00 - max = 0.25
	6+ plrs	0.05 on each $1.00 - max = 0.50
0.50/1.00	2 plrs	0.10 on each $2.00 - max = 0.50
	3-5 plrs	0.10 on each $2.00 - max = 1.00
	6+ plrs	0.10 on each $2.00 - max = 1.50
1.00/2.00	2 plrs	0.25 on each $5.00 - max = 0.50
	3-5 plrs	0.25 on each $5.00 - max = 1.00
	6+ plrs	0.25 on each $5.00 - max = 1.50
2.00/4.00	2 plrs	0.25 on each $5.00 - max = 0.50
	3 plrs	0.25 on each $5.00 - max = 1.00
	4-5 plrs	0.25 on each $5.00 - max = 2.00
	6+ plrs	0.25 on each $5.00 - max = 3.00
3.00/6.00	2 plrs	0.25 on each $10.00 - max = 0.50
	3 plrs	0.50 on each $10.00 - max = 1.00
	4-5 plrs	0.50 on each $10.00 - max = 2.00
	6+ plrs	0.50 on each $10.00 - max = 3.00
4.00/8.00	2 plrs	0.25 on each $10.00 - max = 0.50
	3 plrs	0.50 on each $10.00 - max = 1.00
	4-5 plrs	0.50 on each $10.00 - max = 2.00
	6+ plrs	0.50 on each $10.00 - max = 3.00
5.00/10.00	2 plrs	0.50 on each $20.00 - max = 0.50
	3 plrs	0.50 on each $20.00 - max = 1.00
	4-5 plrs	1.00 on each $20.00 - max = 2.00
	6+ plrs	1.00 on each $20.00 - max = 3.00

THE LAW

As noted in Chapter 1, online gambling is legal if the state in which *you* live or play allows it. Because only Nevada and a few municipalities allow it—or regulate it—all online poker-room servers are physically located outside of the United States, which puts it outside of federal jurisdiction. It's considered offshore gambling. Most experts believe that federal and state governments won't ignore the billions of dollars of potential taxation much longer and that online gambling will become legal online gaming. Until then, millions of real-money online poker players are breaking the rarely enforced laws. It's a personal decision.

ONLINE SECURITY

How safe are online poker rooms and the financial information that you share with them? Most are very safe. Electronic banking has been a way of life for more than a decade and none of these online poker rooms or banking services wants its security system to become headline news. They use secure servers and proven encryption systems, and continuously monitor transactions for breaches. And if breaches ever do occur, chances are they will be in the extremely high-stakes games with big-money players, not where most players play. With adequate personal security measures, playing online with real money is no less secure than playing at a casino. And the rooms are less smoky.

CONTINUED ON NEXT PAGE

Note that a few startup poker rooms have folded, taking players' money with them. It's a chance you take doing business with any business, especially one offshore. If you play for money online, be cautious. Use rec.gambling.poker and other online resources to verify a poker room's trustworthiness before playing for real money. As your bank account grows, make frequent withdrawals to minimize loss. Keep good records. Play smart.

Money in Online Poker

PLAY MONEY

If you decide to play poker online for "play" money, the poker room will give you a specific number of chips, typically 500 or 1,000, as your initial stake. You can then login and play at the "play" tables. For many online poker players, that is enough. In fact, an estimated 75 percent of all online players primarily play these tables and never lose or win a dime.

What is really nice is that if you "lose" all your chips, you can "buy" more chips (at no cost), even during a game, and continue playing.

The third column of the chart shows real money and play money games. The play money games have the word "play" in front of the stake numbers. The seventh column of the chart shows the percentage of players who are still in the game at fourth street.

Table	Game	Stakes	Limit	Plrs	Avg Pot	Plrs/4th	Wait
Power	7 Stud	$1/$2	Fixed	0/8	$4	100%	0
Bulls	7 Stud H/L	$1/$2	Fixed	0/8	$0	0%	0
Aeros	5 Stud	$1/$2	Fixed	0/8	$0	0%	0
Wave	7 Stud	$2/$4	Fixed	0/8	$0	0%	0
Force	7 Stud H/L	$2/$4	Fixed	0/8	$0	0%	0
Peaches	5 Stud	$2/$4	Fixed	**3/8**	$4	72%	0
Captains	7 Stud	$3/$6	Fixed	0/8	$0	0%	0
Gauchos	7 Stud H/L	$3/$6	Fixed	0/8	$0	0%	0
SkyChiefs	5 Stud	$3/$6	Fixed	0/8	$0	0%	0
51s	7 Stud	$5/$10	Fixed	0/8	$0	0%	0
Mustangs	7 Stud H/L	$5/$10	Fixed	0/8	$0	0%	0
Ragin Cajuns	5 Stud	$5/$10	Fixed	0/8	$0	0%	0
Play 4001	7 Stud	Play 5/10	Fixed	0/8	Play 0	0%	0
Play 5000	7 Stud H/L	Play 5/10	Fixed	0/8	Play 0	0%	0
Play 6000	5 Stud	Play 5/10	Fixed	0/8	Play 0	0%	0
Play 4200	7 Stud	Play 20/40	Fixed	0/8	Play 0	0%	0
Play 5200	7 Stud H/L	Play 20/40	Fixed	3/8	Play 255	95%	0
Play 6200	5 Stud	Play 20/40	Fixed	0/8	Play 0	0%	0
Play 4300	7 Stud	Play 50/100	Fixed	0/8	Play 0	0%	0
Play 5300	7 Stud H/L	Play 50/100	Fixed	0/8	Play 0	0%	0
Play 6300	5 Stud	Play 50/100	Fixed	0/8	Play 0	0%	0

TIP

The author recommends that you play online poker for "play money" before attempting cash games. Each online poker room operates a little differently and you can learn its methods without making costly mistakes. Make sure that the game you select from the game menu (shown) clearly indicates whether the game you are joining is for real or play money.

REAL MONEY

When you're ready to play for real money, you'll need to set up a banking account with the poker room. Depending on the room, you can open up an account with cash, check, credit card, or bank transfer. Note that most credit-card companies charge "cash advance" fees for the money. A few credit-card companies won't allow direct payments to online poker rooms and other gaming transactions. Call your credit card company to determine if they allow direct payments to online card rooms and, if so, how you will be charged.

Most online poker rooms accept deposits (minimum $25) from reputable online banking services such as NETeller, FirePay, and PayPal. To establish an online banking service account, you must submit financial information—including your bank account numbers—over a secure server and wait for them to verify the account. Most will deposit a few cents in your account and then ask you how much was deposited to verify that you have access to the bank account you submitted. Some online poker rooms can establish a direct-deposit account from your bank.

TIP

If you plan to play online poker for money, the first step is to establish an account with an online banking service. For additional information, check the resources section of this book.

CONTINUED ON NEXT PAGE

Free Money

Everyone likes "free" money. Online poker rooms want to develop new customers and encourage play, so most offer some type of signing bonus; a few offer ongoing bonuses.

DEPOSIT BONUSES

Deposit bonuses are offered only to new customers. In most cases, that means you don't have any prior account—play or real—at that online poker room. If you have a play account and decide to deposit some money and turn it into a real-money account, you might not be eligible for the bonus. If in doubt, ask the poker room's customer service department. Some of them can waive this restriction.

The deposit bonus typically is based on a percentage of your initial deposit, ranging from 10 to 50 percent of the deposit with a top limit. However, read the fine print. They won't immediately make the full bonus deposit to your account. You probably will be required to play a specific number of hands for each dollar of the bonus. There also might be time limits. Some sites credit you for every *raked* game that you are in, whereas others require that you contribute something to the rake (make a bet) before you get credit.

Poker Bonus Rules:

If you wish to use your bonus to play in the Poker Room, you must earn 3 Bodog Poker Points for every bonus dollar issued before being eligible for a withdrawal i.e. if you earn a $100 bonus, you must earn 300 Bodog Poker Points before placing a withdrawal. Bodog Poker Points are rewarded based on your amount of play in the poker room and the level of stakes at which you play. For more information about how to earn Bodog Poker Points, visit the Poker section and click on "Bodog Poker Points".

Please visit our help section for more information about depositing.

Bonus programs are intended for recreational bettors only. Professional players or players considered to be abusing the bonus system by any means may have bonuses revoked and be subject to further sanctions, at the discretion of Bodog Sportsbook, Casino and Poker Room management.

RELOAD BONUSES

Online poker rooms also want to encourage ongoing play to keep you on their site instead of looking around for another site's bonuses. The reload bonuses typically are a percentage of the amount of any subsequent deposits you make to your account. Some sites also have monthly bonuses that give you a bonus if you play a specified number of hands during the month. And most online poker rooms offer a referral fee paid directly to your account if you refer a friend who opens a real-money account with them.

10% RELOAD BONUS AT BODOG

Each time you reload your online betting account you're eligible for a **10% Cash Bonus**.

To qualify for this bonus, your deposit must be a minimum of $20 if you deposit online, or $50 if you deposit over the phone. This bonus may not be combined with the 10% Signup Bonus. Once your deposit is processed, your bonus will be available for wagering within 30 minutes. Bonuses are issued for new money only, withdrawing and re-depositing money back into your account will not earn bonuses. You may use your bonus to place bets online in the sportsbook, purchase casino chips or play in the poker room.

RAKE REBATES

Another way that you can get "free" money from online poker rooms is to sign up for a *rake rebate.* That is, you can get back some of any rake you pay on won pots. Really! Of course, there are strings attached, and rake rebates may not be worth the effort if you are playing mini-limit tables a couple of hours a week. For more information on rake rebates, see the reference section of this book.

Rake & Blind Structure

Rake: A service fee collected from hands played in real money games, according to the rake chart below.

Raked hand: A hand that a) a player participates in (dealt cards) and b) has generated at least $0.01 in rake for that player. Generated rake is calculated by dividing the total rake collected in that hand by the number of players who were dealt cards.

Bonus requirements: Players are required to play specified numbers of raked hands in order to release bonuses and/or cash out. Tournament entry fees do not count as raked hands for the purpose of bonus release.

Real money games rake chart

No-Limit & Pot-Limit	# of Players	Pot Size	Maximum
Up to $25 Buy-In	Any	$.05 per $1	$3
$25 Buy-In & Above	2 - 3	$.05 per $1	$1
	4 - 5	$.05 per $1	$2
	6 - 10	$.05 per $1	$3

Online Poker Games and Rooms

Online poker rooms all offer the most popular games: Texas Hold'em, Omaha, and Seven-Card Stud, some with high/low variations. A few rooms add Pineapple, Razz, and other games to draw additional players and to entertain those who are bored with more common games. Some offer Blackjack and other card games to satisfy more players.

Refer to Chapter 3 for stud games and variations, Chapter 4 for the basics of playing Texas Hold'em, and Chapter 5 for Omaha and its high/low variation. Draw poker (Chapter 2) is rarely found at online poker rooms and, if so, it is called Jacks or Better.

Online Poker Rooms

There are more than 50 popular online poker rooms—and even more if you count the *skins,* rooms that are front doors for other poker rooms. CardPlayer.com, for example, is a skin for UltimateBet.com, although it is limited to play money. So you have many options. Which should you choose? Try them all for play money and decide which one you enjoy the most. Just remember that you might not get a real-money deposit bonus if you've played some rooms for play money.

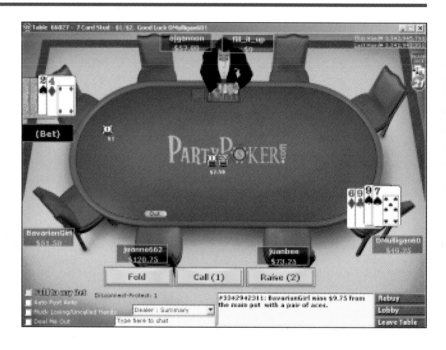

TIP

Playing online poker is similar to playing poker in other venues, except that dealing is much faster. An online poker site typically can deal twice as many games per hour as a physical card room or casino. That's one reason why online playing is increasingly popular among pros and amateurs alike.

PARTYPOKER.COM

Currently the most popular Internet poker room is PartyPoker.com, claiming 75,000 simultaneous players. PartyPoker's servers are located in Gibraltar, a tiny independent country at the southern tip of Spain, where it serves players from around the world. It offers a wide variety of limit and no-limit real- and play-money games, including Texas Hold'em, Omaha, Omaha High/Low, Seven-Card Stud, Seven-Card Stud High-Low, and others.

POKERSTARS.COM

What happens when a handful of World Series of Poker (WSoP) champions get together? They start their own online poker room, PokerStars.com. Second in size to PartyPoker.com, PokerStars is considered first in tournament poker action. In 2003, amateur player Chris Moneymaker paid $40 to enter a PokerStars tournament, a satellite tournament that took him to the World Series of Poker, where he won $2.5 million. Now he's a spokesperson. PokerStars offers the standard poker games with quality graphics.

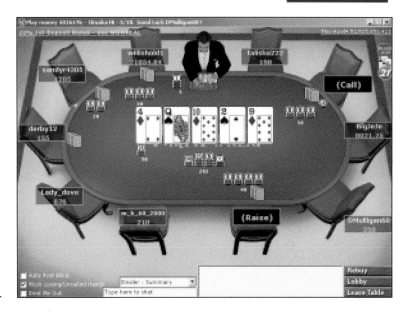

ULTIMATEBET.COM

Another major online poker room is UltimateBet.com, with up to 20,000 players. Games include Hold'em, Omaha, Omaha/8, Seven-Card Stud, Seven-Card Stud/8, Triple Draw, and Pineapple in ring (cash) and tournament games. There are play-money games, too. The graphics are not as flashy as other rooms, but a number of features, including mini-view (minimized view) and player stats, make this a popular site for serious players.

CONTINUED ON NEXT PAGE

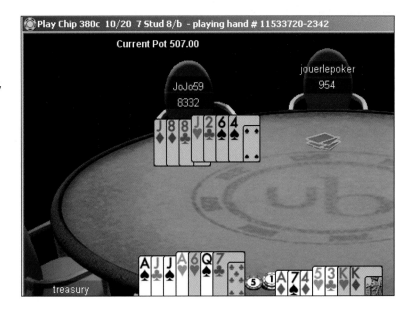

POKERROOM.COM

PokerRoom.com doesn't require that you download player software. Based in Costa Rica, PokerRoom is a popular site for all types of online poker games, offering three-dimensional graphics that make playing more fun. In addition to play and cash-ring games, it has multi-table and sit-and-go tournaments offering the more popular poker games.

BODOG.COM

Bodog.com is a sport betting site that has expanded into the online poker world. Its servers are in Costa Rica. Players can build profiles that help them find and be found by like-minded players. Standard poker games are offered, including real and play money ring games and tournaments.

EMPIREPOKER.COM

Based in Gibraltar, EmpirePoker.com initially served the U.K. and E.U. before expanding worldwide. Games include limit, pot-limit, and no-limit Hold'em, Omaha, and Stud with both high and high/low versions. You must download software for play- and real-money ring and tournament games.

OTHER ONLINE POKER ROOMS

Other popular online poker rooms include PacificPoker.com, ParadisePoker.com, FullTiltPoker.com, MVPpoker.com, ThePokerClub.com, and many more. A free-poker site is available at http://games.yahoo.com. For additional information on these and other online poker rooms, refer to this book's appendix.

What happens if your computer locks up or you lose your Internet connection while playing?
It depends on the site. Some treat lost connections as if the player folded, while others put the player "all in," betting the entire stack. Make sure you know what your online poker room does after disconnects before betting real money.

TIP

There are hundreds of online poker rooms. How can you choose the best one for you? Follow the crowd! Choose one or two of the leading online card rooms, listed in this chapter, and give them a try. But hold off on signing up an account on more than a couple of rooms. Why? Because many rooms offer sign-up bonuses for cash play *if* you don't already have a real or play money account with them.

Online Poker Strategies

Online games are played nearly the same as their card-room counterparts; however, winning strategies are sometimes different. So are the tools that can help you win the pot. In fact, one of the major advantages to playing online (in addition to faster games) is that you can refer to strategy cards, take notes on players, and even use statistics software to help you win. Let's get started!

Poker Tools, Tactics, and Programs

GET INSTANT HAND STATISTICS

Wouldn't it be great to get hand statistics as the game is being played? PokerInspector is a software tool that reads your hole and board cards and tells you how good your hand is compared to possible hands. It even suggests that you check, bet, call, or fold based on a winning profile you create or that PokerInspector shares with you. There are HoldemInspector and StudInspector programs, including demo versions, available at www.PokerInspector.com. Recommended.

In the figure, for example, PokerInspector notes that the player has a straight that is ranked 46 among the 991 possible hands, meaning that only 4.54% of ALL possible hands are better than yours. It then lists the 45 other hands that *could* beat yours. Of course, the program doesn't know what the other hands are yet, but, statisti-

cally, your straight will win most games. Other statistics are available, as well as features that can help you learn poker statistics to the point that you don't need any aids.

Note: *Most poker tool software won't slow down your Internet connection speed.*

GET HAND HISTORIES

Many online poker rooms allow you to request and download complete hand histories that can be read and analyzed offline to learn more about why you or your opponents won or lost. PokerTracker is a software tool that gathers and manages hand histories more easily. You can export the data to a spreadsheet or even to PokerInspector for further analysis.

GET THE ODDS

Other popular software tools can offer odds, percentages, and other useful information to online poker players. And they are allowed by the online poker rooms; they only read and interpret the same data available to all observant players. They just do it *fast!* These tools include PokerInspector, PokerPal, Poker-Spy, Holdem Genius, Poker Indicator, Poker Stove, Poker Sherlock, and many others. Refer to this book's appendix for additional information and resources.

CONTINUED ON NEXT PAGE

GO FISHING

Poker is like fishing. Outsmarting the "fish" (less skillful poker players) can be profitable. When looking for a table at an online poker room, look for one where the higher percentage of players stays to see the flop, fourth street, or another mid-game point. In the illustration, most players will stay to see the flop. Pro players fold poor cards quickly, especially in Hold'em, and poorer players "chase" poor hands to the profit of smarter players. That's where poker profits lurk.

DON'T BELIEVE PLAY MONEY

It's good advice to learn how to play online by beginning with play-money games. However, it's bad advice to play them like they are for play money. Play tight (see Chapter 1), as if each chip is real money. Unfortunately, other players in the play-money games won't be doing that, so there will be more players hanging onto poor cards longer. You will have to adjust to how others play if you move on to real-money tables, but you'll be ready.

For example, in the illustration of a typical online game list, first choose whether you are playing for real or play money. Then choose the game: Omaha or Omaha H/L (high-low). Select the type of game (PL = pot limit, Fixed = fixed limit) and stakes ($0.10/$0.25 up to $10/$20). Consider the average pot and, very important, the percent of players who stay in the game at least until the flop. Selecting the appropriate table is a very important poker skill.

Table	Game	Stakes	Limit	Plrs	Avg Pot	Plrs/Flop	Wait
Red Dogs	Omaha	$0.1/$0.25	PL	1/9	$3	100%	0
Blue Raiders	Omaha	$0.25/$0.5	Fixed	...	$1	100%	0
Dance Smartly	Omaha H/L	$5/$10	PL	0/9	$73	100%	0
Demon	Omaha H/L	$0.5/$1	PL	0/9	$31	87%	0
Paradise Creek	Omaha	$1/$2	PL	1/9	$16	85%	0
Rockets	Omaha H/L	$0.1/$0.25	PL	9/9	$14	84%	0
Wild	Omaha H/L	$1/$2	PL	1/9	$38	80%	0
Utes	Omaha	$5/$10	PL	1/9	$255	80%	0
Boardwalk Bullies	Omaha	$2/$4	PL	7/9	$30	79%	0
Trax	Omaha	$2/$4	PL	6/9	$40	75%	0
Thunderbirds	Omaha	$0.25/$0.5	PL	6/9	$6	72%	0
SuperSonics	Omaha H/L	$0.1/$0.25	PL	7/9	$4	61%	0
Mariners	Omaha	$0.25/$0.5	PL	9/9	$13	61%	0
Phillies	Omaha H/L	$0.1/$0.25	PL	8/9	$4	59%	0
Golden Flashes	Omaha H/L	$0.25/$0.5	PL	9/9	$10	58%	1
Silver Charm	Omaha	$0.1/$0.25	PL	9/9	$5	57%	0
Nets	Omaha	$0.1/$0.25	PL	9/9	$12	54%	0
Red Stockings	Omaha H/L	$0.1/$0.25	PL	9/9	$7	52%	0
Panhandles	Omaha	$0.1/$0.25	PL	9/9	$6	51%	0
Tuneros	Omaha	$0.5/$1	PL	9/9	$18	47%	0
Point Given	Omaha H/L	$1/$2	PL	9/9	$33	46%	1
Forest Oaks	Omaha H/L	$0.1/$0.25	PL	0/9	$0	0%	0
Royal Adelaide	Omaha H/L	$0.1/$0.25	PL	5/9	$0	0%	0

START AT THE LOW-BET TABLES

Once you believe you're ready to graduate to the real-money tables, start small. Play at the nickel and quarter tables to get adjusted to the different way people win and lose at these tables. Better yet, choose a real-money table and observe for a while before joining. You can play well and still lose $25 or more an hour at a $.50 table (shown). Believe me, it's easy!

CHASE BONUSES

Depending on how much free time you have for playing and the room's rules for bonuses, you can play using OPM (*other people's money*) by signing up for the best bonuses and playing the required number and *type* of hands. Make sure you know whether the bonus requires that you participate in the rake or whether you can fold early. Many players build their initial playing pot by looking for or "chasing" the best bonus offers available at various online poker rooms.

CONTINUED ON NEXT PAGE

PLAY AGAINST YOUR COMPUTER

Products such as Wilson Software's Turbo Texas Hold'em (shown) and Turbo Stud offer realistic games against realistic players. In fact, you can select the type of players you battle. They also offer specific hand advice and explanations to help you learn how to win at the money tables without spending a lot of money. Each game can be selected for the betting limits ($20/$40), amounts of the blinds ($10, $20), and the chip colors for various denominations. Demo versions are available for free at www.WilsonSoftware.com.

PLAY AT THE POKER ACADEMY

Another popular software program for learning and playing poker is the Poker Academy, which can be purchased online or in many computer and office-supply stores. In addition to clear instructions, Poker Academy pits you against simulated players for realistic games—and gives you hand advice. Visit them at www.Poker-Academy.com for a free demo version.

DOWNLOAD DEMO OF POKER ACADEMY

The demo version to your right allows you to try Poker Academy Pro free of charge. There are a number of limitations built into the demo that are not present in the full product:

- There are only 100 unique card shuffles, so after 100 hands the cards you play start repeating.
- The showdown calculator allows only one trial hand.
- You cannot add or edit the configuration of tables or opponents.
- You cannot specify board and hole cards to be dealt.
- The demo will expire after two weeks.

 Download Poker Academy Pro Demo for Windows (30MB)

 Download Poker Academy Pro Demo for Mac OS X (25MB)

System Requirements: Windows 98/Me/NT/2000/XP or Mac OS X 10.2.8 (Jaguar) or higher, 128MB RAM, 200MB disk space, 800 MHz CPU.

WHEN IN DOUBT, FOLD

Professional players frequently fold their hands. They say that poker is about winning, but more often it is about *not losing*. For a good example, visit the higher-stakes tables and observe the game for a half-hour or more. You'll quickly determine who the better players are and how frequently they fold. The key to winning poker is, as they say, to "know when to hold 'em and know when to fold 'em." Folding online is easy: simply press the Fold button and your hand will be folded on your next turn.

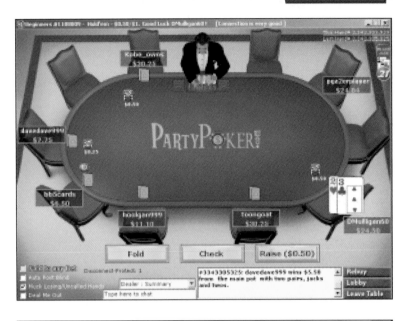

DOUBLE UP

As you get better as an online poker player, you will discover that you are frequently folding bad hands and have extra time while you wait for good hands. Many intermediate players begin playing a second or even a third table, especially if they are using statistic and profile software tools. The three tabs at the top of the online poker room, shown, indicate that the player is simultaneously seated at or visiting three tables. Yes, you will miss some hands you might have won, but your total earnings should be higher. If not, go back to playing one table at a time.

TIP

Tired of fold, fold, fold? Play Royal Hold'em online. It uses a short deck (20 cards) of the Ace, King, Queen, Jack, and Ten in four suits. Every hand is a monster hand, so fewer players fold, pots get fatter, and games often are faster. Most Royal Hold'em games are played as fixed-limit games, but the action is fast and fun.

chapter

8

Play Video Poker

Playing video poker can be fun! Who knows? Maybe your next coin will earn a big payout with lights and whistles! It's worth a coin to find out. Or is it?

This chapter tells you how to win at video poker. It also debunks some of the myths that players have about how video poker works and how to beat it. You'll discover how to spot the winningest machines on the floor and how to play them for a better return. Whether you're a casual player looking for entertainment or a serious player looking for bigger payoffs, you'll discover strategies for winning at video poker.

How to Play Video Poker

Video-poker machines are enticing. How can you pass them and not want to drop in a coin to try your luck? But which one? There might be dozens, even hundreds, of similar video-poker machines lined up in rows on a casino floor. Which one is ready to "pay off"? Which gives the best return for your coin? How can you "outsmart" these machines and win big?

Let's learn more about playing and winning at video poker.

The Game of Video Poker

WHAT IS VIDEO POKER?

First off, video poker isn't poker. The table game of poker is one of skill where winners win money from players with less skill. Video poker pits one player, you, against a machine's preset *payout*. If the machine is set for a 99.5 percent payout, it can return $995 for every $1,000 fed to it. In the short term, it might pay out $1,500 or more; however, in the long term it will average out to $995—or less, because the payout is based on perfect play. Every hand must be played exactly as required based on odds for hand rankings. Payout is explained in greater detail later in this section.

So how can you win playing video poker? Keep reading!

FAQ

What is "perfect play"?

The video-poker machine's preset payout is based on making the mathematically best choice (best odds) of available plays for *every* hand. If you're not a mathematician, practice using software such as Optimum Video Poker (www.OptimumPlay.com) and VPCalculator (www.GambleCraft.com).

THE GAME

A number of popular "poker" games are played on video-poker machines, each with its own rules and strategies. They are covered later in this chapter. The game is played as one person against the machine. Once you select a machine, you insert coins or bills (or an electronic play card) and press the DEAL/DRAW button. Based on the randomly "dealt" cards, you then select any or all of the five cards to HOLD and spin the reel again. (If you change your mind about which cards to hold before you spin again, pressing a HOLD button again cancels holding that card.) The machine reads the resulting hand and, if it matches the game rules for payout, you receive credits (or coins on older machines) following the payout schedule on the front of the machine.

THE MACHINE

Video-poker games are electromechanical machines. The original slot machines were only mechanical, with reels that were spun by pulling a lever at the side of the machine. Modern machines have electronic buttons and even touch-screens for making bets, "shuffling" the cards, selecting cards to hold, determining winning hands, and paying out.

CONTINUED ON NEXT PAGE

THE PAYOUT

How much is paid for specific hands is indicated on the payout schedule on the front of the machine (shown in the illustration). The ranking of hands is the same as for table poker games (see the section "Ranks" in Chapter 1); however, the payout amount is skewed toward larger bets of more coins (called *full-pay*.) Lower-denomination (called *short-pay*) games typically don't offer as good a payout as larger-denomination games.

EXPECTED VALUE (EV)

Expected value is the return on your "investment." If your chance of winning $100 on a specific machine has an expected value (EV) of 95 or 95%, you should expect that, over time, you will get $95.00 back and the loss or cost is $5.00. In the short-term, however, you may lose all $100 or win many times more. That's what gambling is all about.

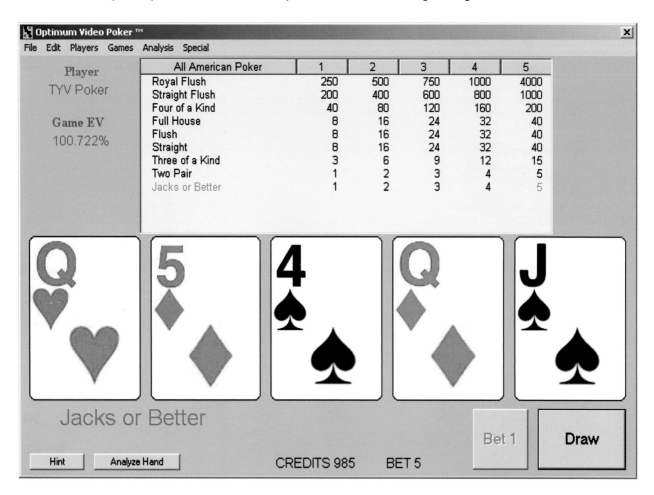

All American Poker	1	2	3	4	5
Royal Flush	250	500	750	1000	4000
Straight Flush	200	400	600	800	1000
Four of a Kind	40	80	120	160	200
Full House	8	16	24	32	40
Flush	8	16	24	32	40
Straight	8	16	24	32	40
Three of a Kind	3	6	9	12	15
Two Pair	1	2	3	4	5
Jacks or Better	1	2	3	4	5

Player
TYV Poker

Game EV
100.722%

Jacks or Better

Hint   Analyze Hand   CREDITS 985   BET 5   Bet 1   Draw

LONG-TERM WINNING

Everyone wants to win more than they bet. The illustration shows the payout for bets of one to five coins.

If video-poker games typically pay out less than they take in, how can a player win? Casinos will give you money to play their games. This "free" money and the resulting winnings are yours to keep. Combining this with playing smart on machines with the highest payback can make you a winner at video poker.

Before putting a single coin into a video-poker machine, go to the casino cashier and sign up for the casino's video-poker or slots club. It's typically free and requires only that you give your name and address. You'll be on the casino's mailing list and will learn about special promotions, free rolls (chances to win drawings without betting money), and other moneysaving opportunities. Before you begin playing, insert your membership card into the machine's card slot and it will keep track of your play.

Note: *Some smaller casinos don't have video-poker or slot clubs.*

Once you've learned how to play and win money at video poker, you can increase your winnings by automating your play. That is, use the MAX BET button to make the maximum bet on the machine (for the highest payout). If the odds are in your favor—due to smart play and good bonuses—play the machines fast for the highest return. An experienced player can play about 500 hands an hour.

Note: *The video-poker screen simulations in this chapter were developed using Optimum Video Poker™. Refer to the "Game EV" calculation on each screen for the game's expected value or return for perfect play.*

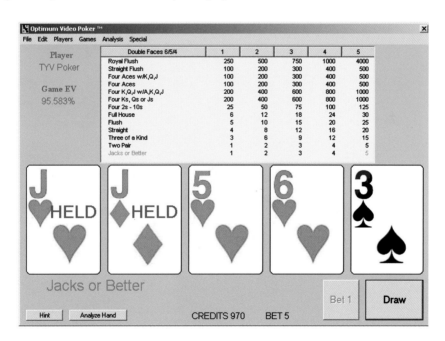

Popular Video-Poker Games

A wide variety of games is available on video-poker machines. Most are based on draw poker (see Chapter 2). Five cards are dealt, one to five are held, replacement cards for non-held cards are drawn, and the final hand is displayed with winning hands indicated by a flashing screen or sounds.

The Games

JACKS-OR-BETTER

Jacks-or-Better is a five-card draw game in which the minimum winning hand is a pair of jacks. The columns show the payout for a specific number of coins bet, from one to five. To select the machine with the best payout, look for a machine with the following payout or better:

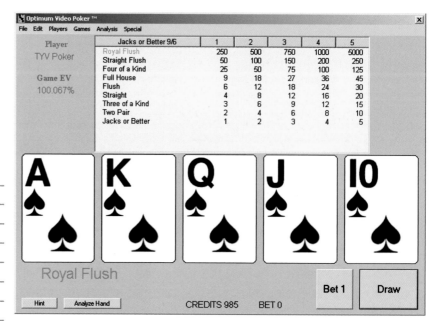

Hand Ranking	Coin Payoff (for Five Coins)
Royal Flush	4,000
Straight flush	250
Four-of-a-kind	125
Full house	**45**
Flush	**30**
Straight	20
Three-of-a-kind	15
Two pair	10
Pair of jacks or better	5

This payout schedule pays nine-for-one for a **full house** (45/5) and six-for-one for a **flush** (30/5) and is referred to as a *9/6 machine.* Read the machine's schedule carefully, however. It might have lower payoffs for other hands. The schedule in the preceding table offers 99.5 percent or better payback on the long term. As a comparison, a 6/5 machine gives the house a 5 percent advantage and pays 95 percent for perfect play.

Which dealt cards should you hold? Following is a proven guideline for Jacks-or-Better video poker, shown below. Hold the highest hand on the list and discard any other cards.

Hands	Examples
Royal or straight flush	A♦-K♦-Q♦-J♦-10♦
Four-of-a-kind	J♥-J♦-J♣-J♠
Full house	8♥-8♦-8♠-4♥-4♦
Four cards to a Royal Flush	A♦-K♦-Q♦-10♦-2♥
Flush	K♠-10♠-8♠-5♠-2♠
Straight	10♦-9♥-8♠-7♠-6♣
Three-of-a-kind	10♠-6♣-3♠-10♠-10♦
Four cards to a straight flush	9♥-8♥-7♥-5♥-Q♠
Two pairs	Q♥-Q♠-7♣-7♥-4♠
Pair of jacks* or better	J♠-J♦-9♣-7♠-2♦
Three cards to a Royal Flush	Q♦-J♦-10♦-9♣-5♠
Four cards to a flush	10♠-8♠-5♠-3♦-2♠
Pair of tens** or lower	10♥-10♦-9♣-7♣-2♦

Hands	Examples
Four cards to an outside straight (four sequential cards that could become a five-card straight)	10♦-9♥-8♠-7♠-3♣
Three cards to a straight flush with no gaps	A♠-9♥-8♥-7♥-5♣
Four cards to an inside straight (four cards that could become a five-card sequential straight)	3♦-4♠-6♣-7♥-J♠
Three cards to a straight flush with one gap	A♠-9♥-8♥-6♥-2♣
Two cards (pair) of jacks* or higher ranking	K♦-K♠-9♥-5♣-4♣
One card jack* or higher ranking	A♦-10♠-8♥-6♠-5♠
Three cards to a straight flush with two gaps	J♥-9♥-8♥-6♥-2♣

Note: * = strategy for Jacks-Or-Better video poker. ** = strategy for Tens-Or-Better video poker.

TENS OR BETTER

A variation on Jacks-or-Better is Tens-or-Better video poker, in which the minimum winning hand is a pair of tens. Select a machine with a 9/6 or better payoff, meaning that a full house pays back nine coins and a flush pays back six coins for one coin bet. Use the above hand chart, except hold a pair of tens or higher, as marked with (**).

CONTINUED ON NEXT PAGE

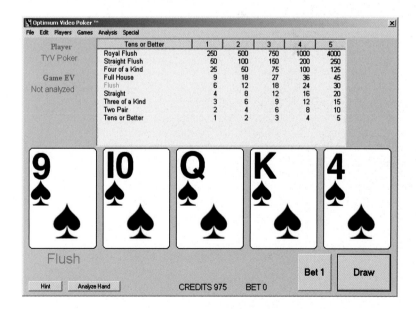

DEUCES WILD

Want to play a game with a long-term payback of 100 percent or more? Play Deuces Wild video poker. Because deuces or twos can be used as any other card, potential winning hands are different than standard rankings. And there are four of these *wild* cards (which can be used as any other card) in each deck. The payout chart has no payoff for a high pair (AA, KK, QQ) or two pair. However, there are bonuses—such as for a hand with four deuces—that more than make up for it. Look for a Deuces Wild machine with the following payout or better:

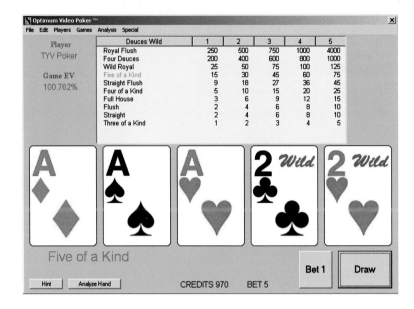

The short-term moneymaking hand in Deuces Wild is four of a kind (*quads*). The payout is a fraction of what quads get in Jacks or Better; however, with four deuce wild cards in the deck, you'll hit quads more often.

Hand Ranking	Coin Payoff (for Five Coins)	Example
Royal Flush	4,000	A♠-K♠-Q♠-J♠-T♠
Four deuces	1,000	2♣-2♦-2♥-2♠-A♠
Wild Royal Flush	125	A♠-K♠-Q♠-J♠-2♠
Five-of-a-kind	75	Shown in the figure.
Straight flush	45	T♦-9♦-8♦-7♦-2♦
Four-of-a-kind	25	T♦-T♠-2♥-2♣-A♠
Full house	15	J♠-J♦-2♣-9♥-9♠
Flush	10	A♠-9♠-6♠-4♠-2♦
Straight	10	Q♥-J♦-T♣-9♠-2♣
Three-of-a-kind	5	K♠-K♦-2♥-8♣-4♦

What dealt cards should you hold? Following is a proven guideline for Deuces Wild. The easy-to-remember rule of Deuces Wild is to keep all your deuces. Beyond that, here's how to play:

Number of Deuces	Keep	Example
Four	All five cards	A♠-2♣-2♦-2♥-2♠
Three	Wild Royal Flush	A♠-K♠-2♣-2♥-2♦
	Five-of-a-kind	K♠-K♦-2♣-2♠-2♥
	Three deuces only	10♥-5♣-2♣-2♠-2♥
Two	Four-of-a-kind or better	6♣-6♠-2♦-2♥-A♠
	Four cards to a Royal or straight flush	A♠-2♠-Q♠-2♦-T♠
	Two deuces only	10♥-5♣-7♣-2♠-2♥
One	Four-of-a-kind or better	T♦-T♣-T♠-2♥-7♣
	Four cards to a straight flush	9♥-8♥-2♥-5♥-Q♠
	Three cards to a Royal Flush	Q♦-J♦-2♦-7♣-5♠
	Any winning hands	
	One deuce only	K♠, 10♥ 8♣, 6♦, 2♠

Number of Deuces	Keep	Example
None	Five or four cards to a Royal Flush	A♣-K♣-Q♣-J♣-9♠
	Any winning hands	
	Four cards to a straight flush	9♥-8♥-7♥-5♥-Q♠
	Three cards to a Royal Flush	Q♦-J♦-10♦-9♣-5♠
	Any pair (not two pairs)	
	Four cards to a flush	10♠-8♠-5♠-3♦-2♠
	Four cards to an outside straight	10♦-9♥-8♠-7♠-3♣
	Three cards to a straight flush	A♠-9♥-8♥-7♥-5♣
	Four cards to an inside straight	3♦-4♠-6♣-7♥-J♠
	Two cards to a Royal Flush	Q♦-J♦-10♣-7♠-3♠

JOKERS WILD

Jokers Wild is similar to Deuces Wild except that the Joker card, not used in most table poker games, is wild and can be used as any other card. Also, there are only two Jokers in a deck, so there are fewer wild cards available to you. If you have one Joker, hold it and any other cards that are winning hands. For example, if you are dealt a pair of sixes and a Joker, hold all three cards for three-of-a-kind. If you were not dealt any Jokers, follow the guidelines for Jacks-or-Better.

CONTINUED ON NEXT PAGE

ALL-AMERICAN POKER

All-American Poker is simply draw poker that pays out eight coins on a full house, flush, or straight for every coin bet. For example, in the figure, the full house (aces full of kings) pays out eight coins for each coin bet, up to 40 coins for a five-coin bet.

All American Poker	1	2	3	4	5
Royal Flush	250	500	750	1000	4000
Straight Flush	200	400	600	800	1000
Four of a Kind	40	80	120	160	200
Full House	8	16	24	32	40
Flush	8	16	24	32	40
Straight	8	16	24	32	40
Three of a Kind	3	6	9	12	15
Two Pair	1	2	3	4	5
Jacks or Better	1	2	3	4	5

DOUBLE DOUBLE BONUS

Double Double Bonus video poker pays out 160 coins on four aces, 80 on four deuces through fours, and 50 on four fives through kings, as shown in the payout in the figure. Some versions pay 10 on a full house (shown), whereas others pay only eight coins.

Double Bonus Poker 10/7	1	2	3	4	5
Royal Flush	250	500	750	1000	4000
Straight Flush	50	100	150	200	250
Four Aces	160	320	480	640	800
Four 2s, 3s or 4s	80	160	240	320	400
Four 5s - Ks	50	100	150	200	250
Full House	10	20	30	40	50
Flush	7	14	21	28	35
Straight	5	10	15	20	25
Three of a Kind	3	6	9	12	15
Two Pair	1	2	3	4	5
Jacks or Better	1	2	3	4	5

DOUBLE DOUBLE JACKPOT

Double Double Jackpot video games pay 160 coins on four aces, and double it if the *kicker* (high-ranking extra card) is a king, queen, or jack. It pays 80 coins for four kings, queens, or jacks, and doubles it if the kicker is an ace, king, queen, or jack.

Double Double Jackpot 10/7/4	1	2	3	4	5
Royal Flush	250	500	750	1000	4000
Straight Flush	50	100	150	200	250
Four Aces w/K,Q,J	320	640	960	1280	1600
Four Aces	160	320	480	640	800
Four K,Q,J w/A,K,Q,J	160	320	480	640	800
Four Ks, Qs or Js	80	160	240	320	400
Four 2s - 10s	50	100	150	200	250
Full House	10	20	30	40	50
Flush	7	14	21	28	35
Straight	4	8	12	16	20
Three of a Kind	3	6	9	12	15
Two Pair	1	2	3	4	5
Jacks or Better	1	2	3	4	5

Player TYV Poker
Game EV 101.249%
Four Aces w/K,Q,J
Hint   Analyze Hand   CREDITS 965   BET 0   Bet 1   Draw

JOKERS WILD (KINGS)

Jokers Wild (Kings) is draw poker with a pair of kings or better required to win. The two Joker cards can substitute for any cards, offering a five-of-a-kind and other winning combinations (shown in the figure). For optimum payout, make sure that four-of-a-kind pays 20 coins and a full house pays seven coins on a one-coin bet.

CONTINUED ON NEXT PAGE

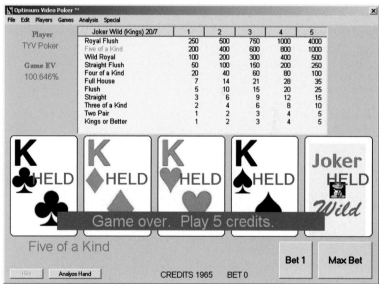

Joker Wild (Kings) 20/7	1	2	3	4	5
Royal Flush	250	500	750	1000	4000
Five of a Kind	200	400	600	800	1000
Wild Royal	100	200	300	400	500
Straight Flush	50	100	150	200	250
Four of a Kind	20	40	60	80	100
Full House	7	14	21	28	35
Flush	5	10	15	20	25
Straight	3	6	9	12	15
Three of a Kind	2	4	6	8	10
Two Pair	1	2	3	4	5
Kings or Better	1	2	3	4	5

Player TYV Poker
Game EV 100.646%
Five of a Kind
Game over.   Play 5 credits.
Hint   Analyze Hand   CREDITS 1965   BET 0   Bet 1   Max Bet

JOKERS WILD (TWO PAIR)

Jokers Wild (Two Pair) requires two pairs or better to win any coins. Jokers are the wild cards. The better-paying machines pay out 5,000 coins instead of 4,000 on a five-coin bet. The figure shows the top winning hand, a Royal Flush that pays 250 coins for each coin bet, with a big bonus (3750 extra coins) for a five-coin bet.

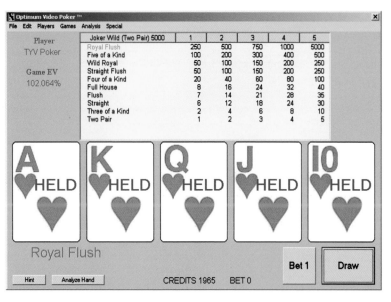

Joker Wild (Two Pair) 5000	1	2	3	4	5
Royal Flush	250	500	750	1000	5000
Five of a Kind	100	200	300	400	500
Wild Royal	50	100	150	200	250
Straight Flush	50	100	150	200	250
Four of a Kind	20	40	60	80	100
Full House	8	16	24	32	40
Flush	7	14	21	28	35
Straight	6	12	18	24	30
Three of a Kind	2	4	6	8	10
Two Pair	1	2	3	4	5

Player TYV Poker

Game EV 102.064%

Royal Flush

LOOSE DEUCES

In Loose Deuces, four-of-a-kind pays four coins for one—unless the quad is four deuces (shown), when the payout is 500 coins for 1. For the best return, make sure that five-of-a-kind pays 15 for 1 and a straight flush pays 10 for 1. Watch for games that have higher payouts or bonuses for maximum bets.

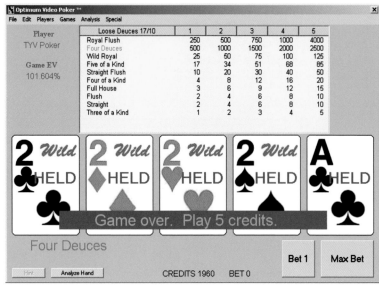

Loose Deuces 17/10	1	2	3	4	5
Royal Flush	250	500	750	1000	4000
Four Deuces	500	1000	1500	2000	2500
Wild Royal	25	50	75	100	125
Five of a Kind	17	34	51	68	85
Straight Flush	10	20	30	40	50
Four of a Kind	4	8	12	16	20
Full House	3	6	9	12	15
Flush	2	4	6	8	10
Straight	2	4	6	8	10
Three of a Kind	1	2	3	4	5

Player TYV Poker

Game EV 101.604%

Four Deuces

Game over. Play 5 credits.

The Easiest Games to Win

According to video-poker expert Dan Paymar, the following games pay 100 percent or more for perfect play:

Game	Expected Value (EV)
Jokers Wild (Two Pair) 5000	102.064%
Jokers Wild (Two Pair)	101.669%
Loose Deuces 17/10	101.604%
All-American Poker 250	101.461%
Double Double Jackpot 10/6/5	101.424%
Double Double Jackpot 10/7/4	101.249%
Deuces Wild 4700	101.076%
Loose Deuces 15/10	100.97%
Bonus Deuces	100.947%
Jacks or Better 9/7	100.8%
Deuces Wild	100.762%

Game	Expected Value (EV)
All American Poker	100.722%
Jacks or Better 10/6	100.695%
Jokers Wild (Kings) 20/7	100.646%
Deuces Wild Double Play	100.606%
Double Bonus Poker SF80	100.519%
Double Double Bonus 9/6/5	100.347%
Double Double Bonus 9/7	100.318%
Double Bonus Poker 10/7	100.173%
Loose Deuces 15/8	100.15%
Double Double Bonus 10/6	100.067%

Dan Paymar's Optimum Video Poker software program (www.OptimumPlay.com) offers practice play and strategies for more than 45 popular video-poker games. I heartily recommend it.

Video-Poker Strategies

The goal of playing poker is winning. Even though you aren't playing video poker against other players, you still can win by joining a player's club, selecting machines with the best payout, and knowing how to play the perfect game. In addition, here are some proven strategies for turning quarter rolls into dollar bills the next time you play video poker.

How to Better Your Chances of Winning

ASK ABOUT PAYBACK

Gaming casinos have video technicians who service machines and answer questions of patrons. Ask a video tech or floor person for the payout percentage of various types of machines. They cannot and will not tell you which machine to play, but they can give you information that will help you make the best decision.

PLAY THE BEST PROGRESSIVES

A *progressive* jackpot is one in which a player who gets the highest possible hand, typically a Royal Flush, is paid a higher-than-standard jackpot. A small percentage of each bet is added to the progressive jackpot. Pros say that the progressive jackpot for a Jacks-or-Better video-poker machine should be at least three times the standard payout for a Royal Flush. Machines with progressive jackpots will have well-lit signs on them announcing that they are "Progressive"—and many also include a current total of the progressive jackpot.

VENUES ARE NOT EQUAL

Gaming is regulated—and taxed. The regulators set the minimum payout allowed for various slot and poker machines. In addition, competition dictates the payout. For example, Las Vegas video-poker games must pay out at least 75 percent; however, extensive competition increases that to nearly 100 percent. Games that have high returns, typically over about 90 percent, are commonly called *loose slots.* Casinos make their money on a small fraction of each bet plus poorly played hands. Indian casinos have different requirements. Casinos on cruise ships are the least regulated because they are open only while the ship is in international waters, so their payout percentage typically is the lowest. Odds are that you won't pay for the cruise with winnings from cruise-ship video-poker games.

PLAY MAX BET

For most video poker games, the casino gets the lowest house odds—and you get the best winning odds—when you play the maximum bet. Most video-poker machines have a MAX BET button that you can select, typically located on the front near the DEAL button to make it easier for players to hit the MAX BET button first.

Max bet button

DROP THE KICKERS

Kickers are useless cards held in hopes of a match, such as an ace or king. Pro players typically don't hold kickers—except when playing Double Double Jackpot games.

CONTINUED ON NEXT PAGE

Video-Poker Strategies *(continued)*

TWO TYPES OF PAIRS

There are only two types of pairs in many video-poker games, a pair of openers (jacks, queens, kings—shown—or aces) and a pair of non-openers (any other pair). A pair of tens (shown), for example, has no greater value than a pair of threes. Remember: You are not playing against the hand of another player; you are playing against the video-poker machine's payout schedule.

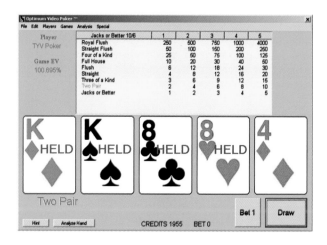

USE STRATEGY CARDS

The games and strategies in this chapter are only the tip of the iceberg. There are dozens of variations to video poker, with many new ones coming out all the time. Rather than lose money to confusing rules, buy a proven strategy card for the specific game you are playing and stick to it. You can purchase video and other poker strategy cards at gambling bookstores and novelty shops. See the Appendix Resources section.

WATCH YOUR MAIL

Once you join a casino slot or video-poker club, get on the mailing list to receive additional benefits. Some offer bonus play, special members-only events, video-poker tournaments with guaranteed prizes, and other opportunities to increase your winnings and fun.

LEARN FROM THE PROS

There are numerous resources available to you that will help you learn more—and win more—at video poker. For further help, visit www.wizardofodds.com and www.advantageplayer.com.

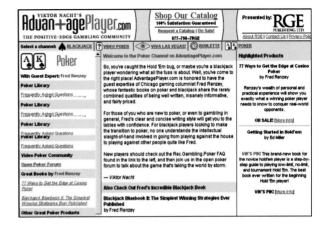

PLAY AT HOME

There are realistic software programs available that let you play video poker at home, such as Optimum Video Poker software, mentioned earlier. Whether you would rather play in a smoke-free environment on your own schedule (without spending much) or you want practice for winning more money, consider video-poker software.

TIP

Check your newspaper's travel section for gaming junkets, trips to casinos offering travel expense refunds in the form of free play and accommodations.

Play Casino Poker

Gaming is big business! The American Gaming Association reports that there were 445 commercial casinos in 11 states generating nearly $29 billion in gross gaming revenue in 2004. And it keeps getting bigger, employing nearly 350,000 people.

Poker is the fastest-growing segment of gaming, with more than $150 million bet in Nevada and New Jersey casinos alone. Add in the 446 card rooms in five states and the grand total tops $1 billion, with the numbers increasing 20 to 45 percent a year! It's being called the "poker phenomenon."

Yet many people who play poker at home, online, or at video-poker machines are reluctant to sit down at a casino card table. They think that other players will quickly attack their chip stack and send them packing back to the slot machines.

It won't happen! If you've learned the rules and nuances of poker, you can easily transition to playing in a casino. This chapter shows you how!

Play Casino Poker

Glitz can bother the eyes and ears. All those flashing lights, sirens, and noisy slot machines are entertainment to some, but a nuisance to others who are trying to concentrate. That's why you won't see as much glitz in the card rooms as you will in casinos where many types of betting games are played. In fact, at many California-style card rooms you won't see *any* glitz. The game is poker and the attitude is serious. Let's win some money!

Similarities and Differences

The biggest difference between playing in a card room and playing on poker machines is that in card rooms you are playing against real people. For standard poker, you are *not* playing against the house (the casino or card room); you aren't playing against a payout chart that, at best, offers you a one or two percent profit for perfect play. You usually are playing against real live people who have more—or less—knowledge, skill, luck, and money than you do. If you have a sufficient bankroll and can play better, overall you will come out on the winning side.

CASINO CARD ROOMS

Larger casinos have their own card rooms and some have many, dedicated to one or a group of games. You'll see blackjack tables and many similar table games in casinos; however, the majority of the rooms are dedicated to poker. It's the latest hot game.

Casinos that provide card rooms, tables, bankers, and dealers are paid a percentage of the amount of money wagered at the table, called the *rake*. A placard at the table identifies the game, the limit (if any), and the rake or house fee for playing.

Some card rooms get paid by a rake taken from each pot by the dealer. However, many card rooms charge the players a rental fee for their seat, periodically taking a *collection* before play can continue. The rake or fee for each table is indicated on a table placard or on a house rules placard near the card club door.

CONTINUED ON NEXT PAGE

Card-Room Etiquette

Although the games are similar, the etiquette for playing at home and at card rooms is different. In most home games, players usually trust each other not to cheat at cards. Playing with strangers in a card room means players assume that everyone will cheat if given the opportunity, so those opportunities are removed. The banker handles all money. The dealer handles all cards and chips (shown) except those "owned" by the individual players. The players can handle only their own private (hole) cards and their own chips. Everyone must play by the rules.

NO SPLASHING

In home games, the pot of chips (or cash) is in the middle of the poker table and each player is trusted to accurately add chips to the pot, called *splashing.* In casino and card-room games, the player places the bet chips in front of him or her, about halfway between their own chips and the main pot. Some poker tables have a bet line (shown) and any chips on the dealer's side of the line are considered bets. Players *do not* directly add chips to the pot. Once individual players have made bets and all active players are equally invested in the pot, the dealer moves the players' bet chips into the pot.

BURNING CARDS

In some card-room games, the dealer is required to *burn* or remove a card from play between deals. Once the initial round of cards is dealt, the first card off the deck in each subsequent round is placed under a chip in the pot as a security measure to show all players that the dealer doesn't somehow take a look at it. It's called the *burn card.*

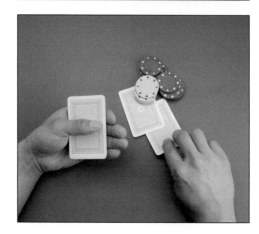

HIDE YOUR CARDS

In many friendly games, the player's hole cards are held in the hand and referred to as needed. To ensure that no player replaces a hole card with another one (*up their sleeve*), all hole cards in casinos and card rooms must remain in contact with the table, face down, until the showdown or until the player folds. Players use their hands to block view of the cards as they lift one corner to see what cards they hold. Professional players usually look at their cards only once and remember them.

DEALER TALK

In many casino and card-room games, the dealer not only deals the cards, but announces what hands the players are showing: "pair of queens," "possible flush," and so on. The dealer also announces the winning hand(s) at showdown and distributes chips to the winner(s).

TOKING

The dealer's salary is paid by the card room or casino. He or she receives *no* income directly from the pot—unless winning players wish to *toke* or tip the dealer one or more chips at the end of a game or when leaving the table. Watch other players to determine an appropriate amount of toke, if any.

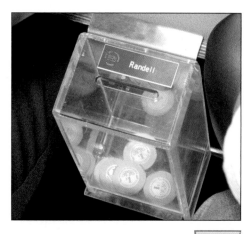

Popular Casino Poker Games

Because casinos and card rooms don't directly profit from the bets, they don't play favorites. These poker games pay the house rent for the space and the dealer, so the house wants to make sure there are sufficient tables available for whatever the *players* want to play. That's good for you. If there are sufficient players who want a specific game, you can bet that the card room will have a table for it.

In addition, note that standard casino poker games pit you against other players; however, some (Three-Card poker, Let It Ride, and Pai Gow) are house games and the odds of winning are lower.

Standard Casino Poker Games

The most popular casino and card room games are Five-Card Draw, Seven-Card Stud, Texas Hold'em, and Omaha, each covered in greater detail in previous chapters. Other popular games include Three-Card Poker, Let It Ride, and Pai Gow, explained below.

FIVE-CARD DRAW

Draw poker was one of the earliest forms of poker (see Chapter 2) and is played at many card rooms and some casinos. The most popular version is Jacks-or-Better, although there are many variations. If you prefer this game, check out local casinos, especially smaller ones, for Five-Card Draw poker. Refer to the posted House Rules card (shown) for specific game information.

Note: *You will rarely find draw poker games with wild cards played in casinos and card rooms.*

SEVEN-CARD STUD

Still a very popular game, you can find Seven-Card Stud in most card rooms and nearly all larger casinos. Refer to Chapter 3 for the specifics of how to play and how to win at Seven-Card Stud. An increasingly popular version of Seven-Card Stud played widely is Seven-Stud/8 (see Chapter 3). Players attempt to build the highest- or lowest-ranking hand at the table, building large pots that are split among the winners.

TEXAS HOLD'EM

The most popular poker game today—and for the past two decades—is Texas Hold'em (see Chapter 4). It's played for high-ranking hands only, and is easy to learn. Because it is considered an entry-level game, be aware that many experienced players, sometimes referred to as *sharks,* are at the casino and card-room tables looking for *fish* (inexperienced players) to devour. Their goal is to trade their education for other players' money.

OMAHA

A variation of Texas Hold'em, Omaha (see Chapter 5) has a different winning strategy and a couple of variations to make it more interesting for poker players. Nine cards are available to each player—four hole cards and five community cards—from which each player attempts to make the best hand of five cards—two from the hole cards and three of the community cards. The variations are that the "best" hand in Omaha is the highest-ranking hand, whereas in Omaha/8 the pot is split between the best high and low hands. Another variation splits the pot between the highest- and lowest-ranking hands.

CONTINUED ON NEXT PAGE

TIP

Most casino card areas have a supervisor who can answer questions about limits and the games played to help you decide which game is right for you.

THREE-CARD POKER

What It Is

Three-Card Poker is a relatively new game that is increasingly popular in many casinos. It's a variation of Stud Poker (see Chapter 3) that presents three ways to bet and four ways to win on your hand. You're playing against the dealer's hand rather than those of the other players, so the games are considered friendlier with lots of chatter among players. Three-Card or Tri Poker is similar to Caribbean Poker and to an older game called "brag." Caribbean Poker typically is played on cruise ships and Three-Card Poker in casinos.

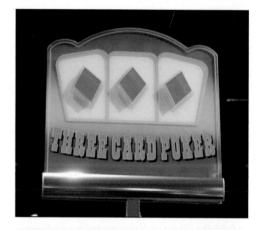

How It's Played

The card table for Three-Card Poker is similar to that for Blackjack, a half-circle with the dealer on one side and six players around the circle. The object of the game is to beat the dealer's hand. The house advantage for many versions of this game is about 2.5 percent, few decisions are needed, and it is fun to play.

Note: A pair-plus bet is one that bets on your hand's value alone. If you have a pair or better, you win. Ante and play bets bet against the dealer.

1. Before any cards are dealt, each player places an ante (an amount between the table minimum and maximum bet) in the ante box and/or the Pair-Plus box marked in front of the player. Most games use an automatic shuffler.

2. The dealer then deals three cards to each player and to the dealer.

3. A player who bets Pair-Plus and is dealt a pair or better gets paid according to the payoff schedule printed on or near the table. If the player's hand beats the dealer's hand (queens or better) the player is paid by the ante payoff schedule.

Three-Card Poker is unique in the rankings of hands because it is easier to get a flush than a straight, as shown in the typical payout schedule on the next page.

Three-Card Poker Payout Schedule

Pair-Plus Pays	
One pair	1 to 1
Flush	4 to 1
Straight	6 to 1
Three-of-a-kind	30 to 1
Straight flush	40 to 1

Ante Bonus Pays	
Straight	1 to 1
Three-of-a-kind	4 to 1
Straight flush	5 to 1

Because Three-Card Poker is a simple game designed for beginning card players, dealers typically are helpful and will give instruction if asked. Some casinos even have regularly scheduled mini-classes on playing these and other house table games.

Winning Three-Card Poker

Here's a winning strategy for Three-Card Poker:

- Always play a hand of Q-6-4 or higher.
- Never play a lower-ranking hand than Q-6-4.

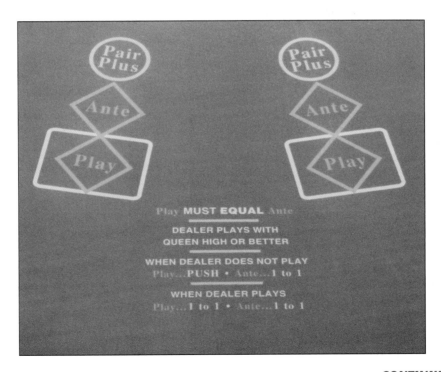

CONTINUED ON NEXT PAGE

LET IT RIDE

What It Is

Let It Ride is another "friendly" casino game where players bet against the house rather than each other. The house advantage in this case is 3.5 percent, meaning that perfect play will return you 96.5 percent of your bets in the long run. Even so, it is a very popular game in many casinos, especially with people who are bored with slots and video poker.

How It's Played

1. Players place equal wagers in the three circles in front of them on the oblong Let It-Ride table.

2. Three cards are then dealt face down to each player; then each player can ask the dealer to remove the first bet (returned to you at the end of the deal) or leave it in place and "let it ride."

3. A single community card is then dealt face up at the center of the table and each player may either have the dealer remove the second bet or let it ride.

4. A second community card is then dealt and players show their cards and are paid according to the Let It Ride payout schedule (see the facing page).

LET IT RIDE PAYOUT SCHEDULE

Payout Schedule for Let It Ride	
Royal Flush	1,000 to 1
Straight flush	200 to 1
Four-of-a-kind	50 to 1
Full house	11 to 1
Flush	8 to 1
Straight	5 to 1
Three-of-a-kind	3 to 1
Two pair	2 to 1
Pair of tens or better	1 to 1

If you have a pair of tens or better, you are paid based on the payout schedule. If not, you lose any bets you did not previously withdraw.

Remember: After you have made your three bets, don't touch the chips until the game is over. The dealer will remove them for you as you direct.

WINNING AT LET IT RIDE

Let It Ride is a relatively simple game with few decisions involved. The payout schedule typically is imprinted on the table and the bet limits are posted near the dealer. The best chance of winning this game is by following the odds of being dealt five cards (see "Card Odds" under "Odds" in Chapter 1) and comparing them to the game's payout schedule.

Here's a winning strategy for Let It Ride:

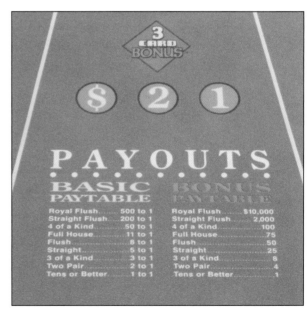

- Let the first circle bet ride if you are dealt a pair of tens or better, three-of-a-kind, a three-card outside straight flush (three cards of the same suit in sequence), a three-card straight flush with one gap and at least one ten or higher (or two gaps and two tens), or any three cards to a royal flush.

- Let the second circle bet ride if your first four cards contain a pair of tens or better, two pair, three-of-a-kind, four-of-a-kind, four cards of the same suit, an outside straight (four cards in sequence), or any four cards to a Royal Flush.

CONTINUED ON NEXT PAGE

PAI GOW POKER

What It is

Pai Gow (pronounced *pie-gow*) Poker is a unique hybrid game that combines the ancient Chinese domino game of Pai Gow with standard poker, with a few twists along the way.

Be aware that in many casinos you are playing Pai Gow against the house's representative, the dealer, rather than against other players. In some casinos, the house takes a five percent rake from which to pay for dealers and glitz, whereas other casinos or card rooms have a house advantage in the odds to pay the bills.

How Pai Gow Is Played

In Pai Gow, you are dealt seven cards from a supplemented deck (52 standard cards plus one Joker). The Joker can be an ace or can complete a straight or flush; it doesn't replace any other cards, however, so it is not truly "wild."

A dice shaker is used to determine which player will be dealt first. Seven cards are then dealt face down to all players, who then sort their hands from highest (H) to lowest (L) to make up a five-card high hand and a two-card low hand, an action called *setting the hands.* The five-card hand must rank higher than the two-card hand. Players are attempting to beat the dealer's high and low hands. If the player beats one of the dealer's hands but not the other, it's called a *push* and no money changes hands.

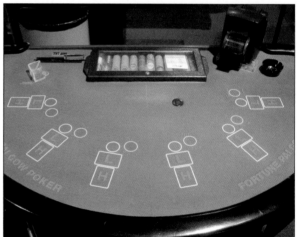

TIP

One way of reducing the house advantage is to become the game's banker. That is, with an adequate bankroll you can become the banker and bet against the other players, paying them off as needed, and reduce the house advantage to about 1 percent. Before attempting to be the banker, make sure you understand the game well and have a large bankroll.

Pai Gow Strategy

Pai Gow hands are ranked similarly to other poker hands
(see Chapter 1), except that the highest hand, beating a Royal
Flush, is five aces—four aces plus the Joker.

One of the advantages to Pai Gow over other forms of poker is
that you can ask the dealer for assistance in setting your cards.
However, don't allow other players to see your hands because
it will give them a betting advantage. In addition, you can ask
the dealer to explain the game to you and answer questions.

Poker is a winnable game. If no one ever won, no one would ever play. Some win by sheer luck, but most win by following a proven strategy for their game. Although each game is different, there are some smart strategies for winning at casino and card-room poker.

BEWARE OF PAYOUT SCHEDULES

As explained earlier in this chapter, some casino games are played against the house and some are played against other players. You typically can tell the difference by looking for a game payout schedule on or near the table. Payout schedules mean you are playing against the house. If in doubt, ask the dealer or banker.

KNOW YOUR MINIMUM BANKROLL

Smart winning means knowing what the odds are for the game. Because odds fluctuate around an average, they might swing dramatically, taking your bankroll from $100 to $1,000 and back again. Many pro players won't step up to a table unless they have 100 bets—$1,000 for a $10-limit table—as their bankroll or stake. The larger the bankroll, the better the chances that they will survive the vagaries of "luck."

SIT BACK AND WATCH

Poker is a game of education. The more you know, the more you can win. But poker isn't an intuitive game, and its many variations make it sometimes difficult to master. The pros watch the game, playing it in their minds, before they ever buy into a specific game. Watching offers a free education that can be invaluable.

OBEY ETIQUETTE

Each poker and casino game has its own etiquette to keep everyone honest and, especially, to keep the game moving. Watching games will teach you the etiquette of the game. So will asking a dealer for instructions. Find a dealer at a slow table and ask her or him to show you how the game is played and how to follow protocol.

WATCH FOR COLLUSION

Sometimes players conspire to gain an advantage, signaling each other toward taking advantage of other players. That's cheating. It typically doesn't happen at low-limit games, but may when the profits are higher. Fortunately, the casino knows all the tricks and has employees watching for collusion between players. If you suspect it, your best bet is to move immediately to another table.

CONTINUED ON NEXT PAGE

KNOW THE PLAYERS

Watching a game for a while before you join it offers the advantage of helping you learn more about how specific players play. You're not as distracted by your own hands and can watch how individuals bet and play their cards. You can watch for *tells* (such as looking away after viewing cards) that you can use once you're in the game to read the player's cards. See "People" in Chapter 1 for more about tells.

KNOW THE CASINO

Where you play can impact how you play. For example, there are many Las Vegas casinos that now have smoke-free poker rooms. Most Indian casinos, however, allow smoking. Rules often are posted near the cashier's cage. Some casinos cater to professional gamblers, whereas others try to draw the occasional gambler or even first-time gamblers (*fish*). Choose your favorite casino or card room as one that reflects your gaming goals.

KNOW YOURSELF

As logical as poker is, many players *tilt* or get emotionally involved in their bets, saying such things as, "I'm feeling lucky tonight" or "I know that the next hand is mine!" and they push all their chips in as an all-in bet. You now know that these feelings in no way change the outcome of the game. Know yourself, understand your emotional side, and keep it away from the poker table for best results.

MANAGE YOUR MONEY

Gaming is about money—more specifically, how much you win. However, the pros know that everyone wins sometime and that the real key to keeping your winnings is not losing. A $100 lead can quickly be eaten up by antes, chases, and bad beats (hands lost to other players' lucky cards). Remember that the dollar you won is a real dollar, just as valuable as any other dollar, so manage it well.

DON'T TILT; HAVE FUN

Taking the game of poker seriously doesn't mean you can't have fun. In fact, gaming is entertainment. It is supposed to be fun. If it isn't, consider another hobby. Just make sure that your fun doesn't confuse your logic. Playing good poker requires that you use both your brain and your spirit to make the game fun—and profitable.

TIP

Many casinos offer free alcoholic drinks to players at some games because it impairs their judgment and causes them to play more emotionally. Most professional poker players avoid alcohol at the table. They don't drink "at work."

chapter 10

Play Tournament Poker

Poker tournaments are hot! Millions of people around the world watch the televised World Series of Poker (WSoP) as it happens each summer. Other international poker tournaments are being played around the world every day of the year. Satellite tournaments feed players—and hope—to millions of poker aficionados. Online poker tournaments draw thousands playing for a seat that might lead to the title of World Champion of Poker.

What are poker tournaments? How do they differ from ring (cash) games? How can *you* get into—and win—a poker tournament? This chapter answers these and many more common questions about the magical world of poker tournaments.

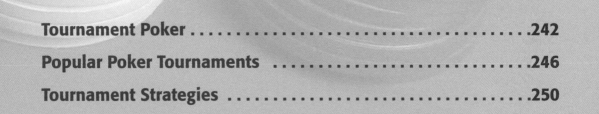

Tournament Poker

Tournament poker has brought new blood—and new money—to the game of poker. What began in Las Vegas 35 years ago as a "friendly" meeting of professional poker players has evolved into a multimillion-dollar industry where new players have a chance to unseat the reigning champion and walk off with major prize money—and bragging rights. What is a poker tournament, anyway? How are they structured and how can you get into one without selling your car and walking to Las Vegas? Let's find out.

Why Play in Tournaments?

For some poker players, tournaments offer benefits over ring games that make them the smarter bet. Tournament players often have more time than money to spend. Tournaments take time to play, from a few hours to a couple of days. But the money at risk typically is lower in tournaments than in ring games. A $20 tournament, for example, might give a player three or four hours of fun playing, whereas a player in a ring game might go through that same amount in an hour or less. A tournament also encourages tighter playing than so-called "play money" or even micro games (limits under a dollar).

If you're sometimes a tilt player, allowing emotions to push you toward making bets that logic says you probably shouldn't make, consider playing more tournaments. You'll probably still lose on the same hands, but at least your losses will be limited to the initial cost to enter, called the *buy-in.* Eventually, tournaments will teach you to play tighter and more logically.

Types of Tournaments

A tournament is a series of contests in competition for a championship. In the case of poker, there are numerous tournaments, large and small, around the world—every day! Some are components of the largest championships, the World Series of Poker or the World Poker Tour (WPT), whereas others end at national or regional championships. Along the way there are many types, styles, and functions of poker tournaments, each with its own requirements and rewards.

The primary types of poker tournaments are elimination, rebuy, shootout, and satellite tournaments.

ELIMINATION TOURNAMENTS

The most common type of poker tournament is structured as an *elimination* tournament. All players buy in at a specified price (for a definition of buy-in, see the section "Tournament Buy-ins") and have the same number of chips to start. . Play continues until one player accumulates all the chips from the other players. Small elimination tournaments have only one table of nine or ten players. Larger tournaments have numerous tables with players vying for a seat at the final table. At the end, the winner receives a previously announced cash prize. Depending on the size of the tournament, other players at the final table also might receive cash prizes.

REBUY TOURNAMENTS

A *rebuy* tournament is similar to an elimination tournament except that players who lose all their chips before a time limit may rebuy more chips and continue to play. Rebuy tournament players play more aggressively because they can get back into the game if they lose everything. Most rebuy tournaments have a time limit for rebuying.

CONTINUED ON NEXT PAGE

SHOOTOUT TOURNAMENTS

Shootout tournaments send the winner of each table on to the final event regardless of their ranking in the total tournament. A less-experienced player at a loose table can get farther in a shootout tournament than in other types of tournaments, maybe even on to the championship chair. Because there is a greater variation in player skills at the final tables, shootout tournaments typically don't last as long as elimination tournaments.

SATELLITE TOURNAMENTS

Satellite tournaments are "mini" or small tournaments where the prize is a seat at a larger tournament. The WSoP and WPT have many satellite tournaments across the country that feed quality players to the main events.

Tournament Buy-ins

To play in tournaments, players pay a fee, called a *buy-in*. Casino and card-club tournaments have buy-ins that range from $20 to $10,000 or more. The WSoP buy-in is $10,000! Of course, the prize pool depends on how many players buy in and at what amount, so it benefits players to get into tournaments with higher buy-ins. For example, in the illustration, the game is no-limit with a minimum buy-in of $100 and a maximum of $300.

But everyone must start somewhere. Online tournaments typically have smaller buy-ins, beginning at just a few dollars. Some online tournaments are bought in with player points earned by playing at the online poker site.

Remember that some tournament buy-ins allow a rebuy within a specified period. Make sure you know the tournament rules and limits before signing up.

Tournament Betting

Tournaments, like ring games, have various betting limits (see Chapter 1), established by the rules. Some tournaments are limit games, such as $10/$20 or $25/$50. Others are pot-limit tournaments. A majority are no-limit tournaments, especially the larger tournaments.

Players select a card from the dealer's spread (shown) to determine who will be the first player, designated as the "dealer." To keep things moving, most tournaments have a *graduated blind structure.* That is, after a specified round, the blinds or antes are increased to reduce the number of active players, especially those with small chip stacks. Simultaneously, the betting limits (if any) are increased. This structure keeps the tightest players from folding every hand but *the nuts* (see Chapter 4). They have to attempt to win a few pots with weaker hands just to replace the chips they lose to paying the blinds or antes.

Tournament Prizes

How much will you win in a tournament? Before entering any tournament, make sure you understand the rules—and the prize pool. For example, if you enter a tournament with a $100 buy-in and it will begin when there are 100 entrants ($10,000 in entry fees), a typical prize schedule will look similar to this:

Tournament promoters aren't magnanimous. Each game will have a table rake or fee that is deducted from the winnings. Alternatively, some tournaments add a fee up front; the entry fee might be $100 + $10 (entry fee or rake), for example. Again, make sure you know the rules before you play the game.

Also note that some tournaments have a "guaranteed" prize pool whereas others don't. The winner of a non-guaranteed tournament gets a percentage of the pool; if there are fewer players signed up than were expected, the winnings are reduced.

Place	Percent of Pool	Winnings
1st	40%	$4,000
2nd	20%	$2,000
3rd	10%	$1,000
4th	6%	$600
5th	4%	$400
6th	3%	$300
7th	2%	$200
8th–22nd	1%	$100 each (return entry fee)
	100%	$10,000

Popular Poker Tournaments

Poker tournaments come in all types, sizes, games, and awards. They are played in small card rooms, large casinos, and even online. The largest one is the World Series of Poker, but there are many others that make tournament play fun for many thousands of poker players worldwide.

World Series of Poker

The World Series of Poker began in 1970 when a group of professional players got together at Binion's Horseshoe Casino in downtown Las Vegas to play a championship tournament. Today, preliminary WSoP tournaments are hosted by Harrah's in Las Vegas and begin more than a month before the final event in mid-July at Binion's.

WSoP doesn't play just Texas Hold'em. Beginning in early June, the first of more than 40 tournaments is seated at 12 P.M. each day. The games are limit, pot-limit, and no-limit Hold'em; short-handed (six players) Hold'em; limit, pot-limit, and no-limit Omaha; Seven-Card Stud High and High-Low Split; Seven-Card Razz (Lowball Stud); and other games. Special tournaments also are played for casino employees, ladies, seniors, and even a celebrity charity event.

The major event of the WSoP is the no-limit Texas Hold'em world championship event played for 10 days in early- and mid-July each year. In 2005 it began at Harrah's Rio Hotel and Casino in Las Vegas. There are four tournaments within the championship, the first with a $10,000 buy-in. The final event, no-limit Hold'em, moves to Binion's Gambling Hall and Hotel for the final tables and crowning of the champion.

TIP

Want to participate in the WSoP? Visit www.WorldSeriesOfPoker.com for the dates, satellite game circuits, event registration and fees, plus info on past winners. You even can purchase souvenirs.

World Poker Tour

Another major tournament series is the World Poker Tour that encompasses dozens of satellite tournaments around the world. On any given day, there is a WPT tournament being held somewhere in a casino, online, or both. Venues range from Jupiter, Florida; and Turlock, California; to the WPT World Championship in Las Vegas in late February. Many WPT tournaments are televised live or delayed, primarily on The Travel Channel network.

Other Major Tournaments

Some of the other large poker tournaments include the following:

- Orleans Open at the Orleans Casino in Las Vegas, Nevada
- Shooting Star at the Bay 101 Casino in San Jose, California
- California State Poker Championship at the Commerce Casino in Los Angeles, California
- 5 Star Classic at the Bellagio Casino in Las Vegas, Nevada
- Legends of Poker at the Bicycle Casino in Los Angeles, California
- Five Diamond World Poker Classic at the Bellagio Casino in Las Vegas, Nevada
- World Poker Finals at Foxwoods in Mashantucket, Connecticut
- L.A. Poker Classic at the Commerce Casino in Los Angeles, California
- Showdown at Sands at the Sands Casino in Las Vegas, Nevada

TIP

Want to participate in the WPT? Visit www.WorldPokerTour.com for the game calendar, satellite game circuits, event registration and fees, and facts about past winners. Souvenirs are available online.

CONTINUED ON NEXT PAGE

Local Tournaments

Most cities and towns are within a couple of hours' drive of a casino, card room, or other poker-tournament venue. And many tournament participants play only locally, never hitting the big prize that takes them on to a regional, national, or international tournament. That's okay.

To find out about poker tournaments in your area, first check the area telephone books for casinos and card rooms. A few telephone calls will get you on some mailing lists or give you Web addresses where you can learn more about local tournament venues and schedules.

Local tournaments usually are more friendly, social events than other types of tournaments. Chances are the players there are people that you have previously played in ring games. So you might find more table chatter at local tournaments than in local ring or regional tournament games. This is especially true of tournaments with low buy-ins that frequently attract newer players.

Some local tournaments also are satellite tournaments for the regional tournaments that feed into the WSoP and WPT tournaments. For example, the WPT includes the Gran Prix de Paris tournament as well as the Los Angeles Poker Classic. The point is that some poker talent and lots of good luck can take you to a seven-digit payday. It has happened!

TIP

Both the WSoP and the WPT include small buy-in tournaments around the world where an initial buy-in of less than $100—and sometimes less than $20—can, eventually, earn you a seat at one of their final tables. Some of the larger online poker rooms, too, have small buy-in tournaments that can lead to a championship—or at least a lot of fun.

Online Tournaments

Don't ignore online tournaments as a way of building your skills and perhaps gaining a seat at a national tournament. Many of the WSoP top winners over the past few years have earned seats by first winning online tournaments. Some rarely played in any casino or card room, just online (see Chapter 7).

There are two types of tournaments at online poker rooms. The *scheduled tournament* requires that you sign up and the first game begins at a specified date and time. Fortunately, there are dozens of such tournaments going on each day at various online poker rooms. For example, in the illustration, you can select your game from a long list of regular or sit-and-go (see below) tournament games.

The newest type of tournament is called *sit-and-go.* These tournaments typically are smaller, with fewer players and only one or two tables. Everyone signs up in advance and the game begins when a specified number of players are signed up. It's a fun way to play in a tournament and gain skill at nearly any hour of the day or night that you want to play. The example in the illustration is of a Seven-Card Stud sit-and-go tournament with a $10 buy-in plus a $1 entry fee, as indicated at the top of the screen.

Tournament Strategies

As in all poker games, players with the best strategies win more frequently. The best strategies are those that are mathematically sound and are proven in real tournaments. Theories don't get you to the final chair. Here are some proven strategies for winning tournament poker.

Advice for Would-Be Tournament Players

ONLY TOP FINISHERS NEED APPLY

Playing in tournaments can be fun, but, as you can see by the typical prize schedule, only the top few winners get much of the prize money. Most others break even or count it as an expense to play in poker tournaments. However, if you don't mind finishing "out of the money," it is still a cheaper hobby than many others.

PLAY SLOW

You win a tournament by keeping your chip stack longer than anyone else. That means playing tighter (only playing the better starting hands) than you might for a ring game. Be continually aware of your chip stack size and that of your opponents at the table. Also learn to read "tells" so that you can make smarter bets. Tournaments without rebuys limit your stake, so you must bet it more wisely.

PLAY AGGRESSIVELY

Once you have *the nuts* (the best possible hand), play aggressively. Push more chips in. A great opening hand can quickly clear a table of second-best hands and build your chip pile. Just make sure that yours isn't second best.

WATCH OTHER PLAYERS' STACKS

All players aren't created equal in ring games. Some bring large chip stacks to the table, whereas others have only the minimum buy-in. For example, the buy-in may be $5 minimum and $100 maximum. In tournaments, however, all players begin with the same number of chips. By watching players' chip stacks and how they play them, you can learn of any weaknesses—such as "bets heavy on suited connectors"—that you can take advantage of later in the game.

BLUFF IN NO-LIMIT GAMES

Poker games in which there is no betting limit require special skills, and the most important one is knowing when and how to bluff. The player on the left may be bluffing by holding chips as if to say to other players, "I'm going to raise your bet." A good bluff can buy you the pot—and a bad bluff can empty your chair. Before playing in no-limit games, make sure you know how to bluff and have successfully practiced. It is a key to winning no-limit tournaments.

CONTINUED ON NEXT PAGE

SURVIVAL OF THE SMARTEST

Tournaments are about surviving to the final table and the final seat. Play tight. Learn to read your opponents. Learn how to psych your opponents. Manage well your limited number of chips. In the photo, the player is playing tight by folding a weak opening hand. Survive!

PUSH ALL-IN

If your opponent has only a few chips left and you think you have the better hand, bet to force the opponent "all in" (run out of chips when betting or calling) to possibly eliminate him or her from the table. Otherwise, the opponent might get very lucky on the next hand and those straggler chips might cost you big.

DON'T CHASE THE BLIND

In Hold'em and Omaha where two players must contribute the small and big blinds, sometimes those players hang onto weak hands because they want to get a little action for their other-wise dead bet. So they call or even raise and hope that the flop (three community cards) helps them. Even after the flop, they probably will still have a weak hand. Instead, let the blind go and win it back later with a strong hand.

CONSERVE YOURSELF

Some poker players naturally come on strong in the first few hands of a game to intimidate other players. This strategy often works well in ring games, but not as well in tournament action. Remember, it's about survival. Play tight, pace yourself, and win in the long haul. The player shown is keeping his chips on his side of the table's betting line.

BUY IN EARLY

Better players often wait until just before the deadline to buy into a tournament because they want to see who they are playing against before committing. Newer tournament players should buy in early and watch the players as they sign up and get seated. The new player also listens carefully to conversations to help analyze the playing styles (see Chapter 1) of other players. Much of winning poker—especially tournament poker—is knowing your opponent.

Shown is a dealer mixing cards before a shuffle.

appendix A

Charts

Visual poker players like charts! Charts can help you play poker smarter and better. This appendix includes hand-ranking and odds charts for popular poker games: Five-Card Draw, Lowball Draw, Seven-Card Stud, Razz, Texas Hold'em, and Omaha.

Good luck at the tables!

Hand-Ranking Charts

Most poker games are played to determine the highest-ranking hand at the table. This chart will guide you; memorize it.

High Ranking

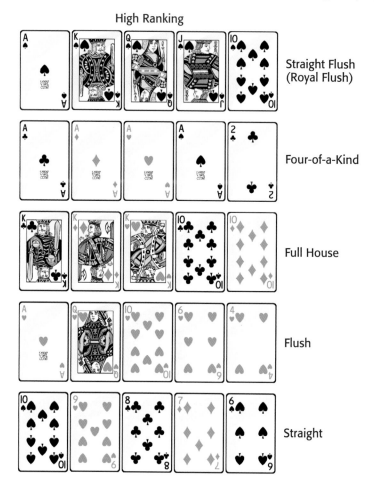

Straight Flush
(Royal Flush)

Four-of-a-Kind

Full House

Flush

Straight

Poker also can be played for the lowest-ranking hand as well. Low games include Lowball Draw, Razz, and Omaha/8. Here are the commonly accepted lowest-ranking poker hands.

Low Ranking

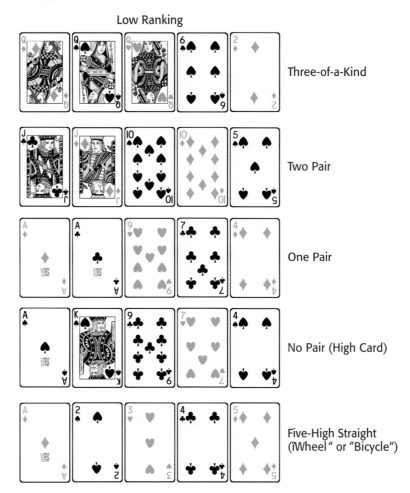

Three-of-a-Kind

Two Pair

One Pair

No Pair (High Card)

Five-High Straight
("Wheel" or "Bicycle")

Odds Charts

Five-Card Draw Poker Odds

Hand	Probability of Being Dealt in Original Five Cards
Royal Flush	649,740:1 (0.00015%)
Straight flush	72,193:1 (0.0014%)
Four-of-a-kind	4,165:1 (0.024%)
Full house	694:1 (0.14%)
Flush	509:1 (0.2%)
Straight	255:1 (0.39%)
Three-of-a-kind	47:1 (2.08%)
Two pairs	21:1 (4.55%)
One pair	2.4:1 (29.4%)
No-pair hand	2:1 (33.33%)

Lowball Draw Poker Odds

Hand	Probability of Being Dealt in Original Five Cards
Wheel or Bicycle (A-2-3-4-5)	2,537:1 (0.04%)
Six-high	507:1 (0.2%)
Seven-high	168:1 (0.59%)
Eight-high	71.5:1 (1.38%)
Nine-high	35.3:1 (2.76%)

Seven-Card Stud Poker Odds for Starting Hands

Hand	Probability of Being Dealt in First Three Cards
3 Aces	5,524:1 (0.02%)
3 Jacks through 3 Kings	1,841:1 (0.05%)
3 Sixes through 3 Tens	1,104:1 (0.09%)
3 Twos through 3 Fives	1,380:1 (0.07%)
2 Aces	75.7:1 (1.3%)
2 Jacks through 2 Kings	24.6:1 (3.91%)
2 Sixes through 2 Tens	14.3:1 (6.52%)
2 Twos through 2 Fives	18.2:1 (5.21%)
Three cards of a straight flush	85.3:1 (1.16%)
Three cards of a flush	23.9:1 (4.02%)
Three cards of a straight	4.76:1 (17.38%)
Three-of-a-kind	424:1 (0.24%)
Pair	4.9:1 (16.94%)

Seven-Card Stud Poker Low (Razz) Odds for Starting Hands

Hand	Probability of Being Dealt in First Three Cards
A-2-3 (lowest possible)	344:1 (0.29%)
Four-low or better	85.3:1 (1.16%)
Five-low or better	33.5:1 (2.9%)
Six-low or better	16.3:1 (5.79%)
Seven-low or better	8.87:1 (10.14%)
Eight-low or better	5.17:1 (16.22%)
Nine-low or better	3.11:1 (24.33%)

CONTINUED ON NEXT PAGE

Odds Charts
(continued)

Texas Hold'em Poker Odds

Hand	Probability
Pre-Flop Starting Hands	
Pocket Aces	220:1 (0.45%)
Pocket Aces or Kings	110:1 (0.9%)
Any pocket pair	16:1 (5.9%)
AK suited	331:1 (0.3%)
AK unsuited	110:1 (0.9%)
Any two suited cards	3.3:1 (24%)
Flop	
With a pocket pair, flopping a set (3)	8.3:1 (10.8%)
With a pocket pair, flopping a full house	136:1 (0.74%)
With a pocket pair, flopping quads (4)	407:1 (0.25%)
With two suited cards, flopping a flush	118:1 (0.84%)
With two suited cards, flopping a flush draw	8.1:1 (10.9%)
With two non-pair cards, flopping to a pair	2.1:1 (32.4%)
With two non-pair cards, flopping to two pair	49:1 (2%)
Turn	
Making a full house from a set	5.7:1 (15%)
Making a full house from two pair	11:1 (9%)
Making a flush from a flush draw	4.2:1 (19%)
Making a straight from an open-ended straight draw	4.9:1 (17%)
Making a pair from two overcards	6.8:1 (13%)
River	
Making a full house or better from a set	3.6:1 (22.7%)
Making a full house from two pair	11:1 (9%)
Making a flush from a flush draw	4.1:1 (20%)
Making a straight from an open-ended straight draw	4.8:1 (17%)

Omaha Poker Odds

Omaha, like many other forms of poker, relies on "outs," or cards that can give you a winning hand. Knowing the outs for your hand and the odds or percentages involved can help you to play smarter and win more.

Outs, Odds, and Percentages (after the Flop)		
Outs	**Odds Against Making by River**	**Percentage Chance of Making by River**
4	4.8:1	17%
5	3.8:1	21%
6	3:1	25%
7	2.4:1	29%
8	2:1	33%
9	1.8:1	36%
10	1.5:1	40%
11	1.3:1	43%
12	1.1:1	47%
13	1:1	50%
14	0.9:1	53%
15	0.8:1	56%
16	0.7:1	59%
17	0.6:1	62%
18	0.5:1	65%
19	0.5:1	67%
20	0.4:1	70%

B

Poker Resources

There's more to learn about poker. In fact, playing good poker is an ongoing education. This appendix suggests some next steps in your poker education: places you can play, online poker games, computer resources, and further reading. Keep learning—and keep winning!

Places to Play Poker

There are thousands of places to play poker, from the neighborhood card room to Las Vegas, to cruise ships and even online. Here are a few.

Casinos with Poker Rooms

ATLANTIC CITY, NJ

Bally's Park Place
Caesar's
Tropicana Casino Poker Room
Trump Marina Hotel Casino
Trump Taj Mahal Atlantic City
Trump Taj Mahal Poker Parlor

LAS VEGAS, NV

Aladdin
Bally's
Bellagio
Binion's
Circus Circus
El Cortez
Excalibur
Flamingo Las Vegas
Gold Coast
Golden Nugget
Harrah's
Imperial Palace
Luxor
Mandalay Bay
Orleans
Palms
Plaza
Rio
Sahara Hotel
Sam's Town
Stardust Resort

RENO, NV

Atlantis Casino Resort
Boomtown Hotel Casino
Circus Circus
Club Cal-Neva
Eldorado Hotel Casino
Flamingo Hilton
Peppermill Hotel Casino
Reno Hilton

OTHER PLACES

By state law, city ordinance, or Native American treaties, poker card clubs currently operate legally within Arizona, California, Colorado, Connecticut, Delaware, Florida, Idaho, Illinois, Indiana, Iowa, Kansas, Louisiana, Michigan, Minnesota, Mississippi, Missouri, Montana, Nebraska, Nevada, New Mexico, New York, North Carolina, North Dakota, Oklahoma, Oregon, South Dakota, Texas, Washington, and Wisconsin. The list is extensive and ever-changing. Check your area telephone books for casinos and poker rooms.

Online and Computer Resources

Many thousands of people are playing poker online right now (although it may be illegal in some locations). Others are catching up on the latest poker news, developing new skills, or just complaining about a bad beat (a hand beaten by a lucky draw). You can, too. In addition, there are many computer tools to help you play smarter and win more. Here are some of the primary resources.

Online Poker Rooms

Pokerpulse.com recently counted 316 online poker rooms. The major rooms include the following:

- absolutepoker.com
- b2bpoker.com
- bet365poker.com
- bodog.com
- cdpoker.com
- celebritypoker.com
- doylesroom.com
- empirepoker.com
- europoker.com
- everestpoker.com
- fairpoker.com
- fulltiltpoker.com
- goldenpalacepoker.com
- holdempoker.com
- hollywoodpoker.com
- interpoker.com
- ladbrokespoker.com

- noblepoker.com
- pacificpoker.com
- paradisepoker.com
- partypoker.com
- poker.com
- pokerhost.com
- pokerplex.com
- pokerroom.com
- pokerstars.com
- pokertime.com
- primapoker.com
- royalvegaspoker.com
- sunpoker.com
- tigergaming.com
- titanpoker.com
- tribecatables.com
- ultimatebet.com
- usapoker.com
- vippoker.com
- visual-poker.com
- williamhillpoker.com

CONTINUED ON NEXT PAGE

Computer Software

Wilson Software offers Turbo Texas Hold'em, Tournament Hold'em, Turbo 7-Card Stud, Turbo Stud 8/Better, Turbo Omaha High-Only, and Turbo Omaha High-Low. Demo copies are available at their website, www.wilsonsoftware.com.

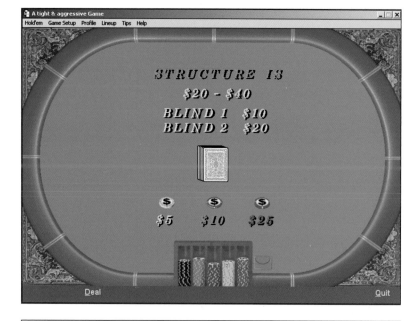

Accidental Software offers FatCat Poker with Five-Card Stud, Seven-Card Stud, High Chicago, Texas Hold'em, Five-Card Draw (Jacks or Better), and Five-Card Draw (No Openers Required). Demo copies of FatCat Poker and other programs are available at www.accidental.com.

Other poker-playing software and tools can be found online at the following sites:

acespade.com
calculatem.com
conjelco.com (StatKing)
ddpoker.com
poker-edge.com
pokerindicator.com
pokerinspector.com
poker-spy.com
pokerstove.com
pokertracker.com
poki-poker.com

No single book can tell you everything there is to know about poker. In fact, all of the books combined can't replace experience. However, when you're not at the table cleaning the "fish," read these and other books on poker and gambling.

On Poker

Caro's Book of Poker Tells by Mike Caro (Cardoza, 2003).

Doyle Brunson's Super System: A Course in Power Poker by Doyle Brunson (Cardoza, 1979).

Doyle Brunson's Super System II by Doyle Brunson (Cardoza, 2005).

Fundamentals of Poker by Mason Malmuth and Lynne Loomis (Two Plus Two Publishing, 2004).

Harrington on Hold'em: Expert Strategy for No-Limit Tournaments (two volumes) by Dan Harrington (Two Plus Two Publishing, 2004).

Hold'em for Advanced Players by David Sklansky (Two Plus Two Publishing, 1999).

Hold'em Poker by David Sklansky (Two Plus Two Publishing, 1997).

How to Beat Low-Limit 7-Card Stud Poker by Paul Kammen (Cardoza, 2003).

How to Play Poker and Other Gambling Card Games by Peter Arnold (Hamlyn, 2003).

Improve Your Poker by Bob Ciaffone (Bob Ciaffone, 1997).

Inside the Poker Mind: Essays on Hold'em and General Poker Concepts by John Feeney, PhD (Two Plus Two Publishing, 2000).

Internet Texas Hold'em: Winning Strategies from an Internet Pro by Matthew Hilger (Matthew Hilger, 2003).

CONTINUED ON NEXT PAGE

Middle Limit Hold'em Poker by Bob Ciaffone (Bob Ciaffone, 2002).

Phil Gordon's Little Green Book: Lessons and Teachings in No-Limit Texas Hold'em by Phil Gordon (Simon Spotlight Entertainment, 2005).

Play Poker Like the Pros by Phil Hellmuth Jr. (Harper Resource, 2003).

Poker For Dummies by Richard D. Harroch and Lou Krieger (Wiley Publishing, Inc., 2000).

Poker: The Real Deal by Phil Gordon (Simon Spotlight Entertainment, 2004).

Seven-Card Stud for Advanced Players by David Sklansky (Two Plus Two Publishing, 1999).

Small Stakes Hold'em: Winning Big with Expert Play by Ed Miller (Two Plus Two Publishing, 2004).

The Complete Book of Hold'em Poker: A Comprehensive Guide to Playing and Winning by Gary Carson (Lyle Stuart, 2001).

The Complete Idiot's Guide to Poker by Andrew N.S. Glazer (Alpha Books, 2004).

The Official Rules of Card Games (The United States Playing Card Co., 1999).

The Poker Book by Peter Arnold (Gramercy Books, 2004).

The Poker Player's Bible: How to Play Winning Poker by Lou Krieger (Barron's Educational Series Inc., 2004).

The Psychology of Poker by Alan N. Schoonmaker, PhD (Two Plus Two Publishing, 2000).

The Theory of Poker by David Sklansky (Two Plus Two Publishing, 1999).

Thursday-Night Poker: How to Understand, Enjoy—and Win by Peter O. Steiner (Ballantine Books, 2005).

Video Poker: Optimum Play by Dan Paymar (ConJelCo, 2004).

Weighing the Odds in Hold'em Poker by King Yao (Pi Yee Press, 2005).

Win at Video Poker: The Guide to Beating the Poker Machines by Roger Fleming (Citadel Press, 1998).

Winning Concepts in Draw and Lowball by Mason Malmuth (Two Plus Two Publishing, 1987).

Winning Low Limit Hold'em (Second Edition) by Lee Jones (ConJelCo, 2000).

Winning Poker: 200 Rules, Techniques & Strategies by Dean Matthewson and Angie Diamond (Black Dog & Leventhal Publishers, 2004).

Winning Secrets of Online Poker by Douglas W. Frye and Curtis D. Frye (Thomson Course Technology, 2005).

On Gaming and Gambling

Gambling For Dummies by Richard D. Harroch, Lou Kreiger, and Arthur S. Reber (Wiley Publishing, Inc., 2001).

How to Gamble at the Casinos Without Getting Plucked Like a Chicken by James Harrison Ford (El Paso Norte Press, 2004).

The Everything Casino Gambling Book by George Mandos (Adams Media, 1998).

Win at the Casino by Dennis R. Harrison (Lifetime Books, 1996).

Poker Magazines

All-in, allinmag.com

Bluff, bluffmagazine.com

Card Player, cardplayer.com

Card Player College, cardplayer.com/cpcollege

Card Player Europe, cardplayer.com/cpeurope

Casino Player, casinoplayer.com

Gambling Times, gamblingtimes.com

Part Time Poker, parttimepoker.com

Poker, pokermagazine.com

Poker Player, pokerplayernewspaper.com

Poker Pro, thepokerpromagazine.com

Poker Web, thepokerweb.com/poker-news.html

Top Pair, toppairmagazine.com

Video Poker Player, vpplayer.com

Woman Poker Player, womanpokerplayer.com

Glossary of Poker Terms

Poker has a language unto itself—from *A-game* to *zombie*. Following are some of the more common poker terms and their concise definitions.

A-game   The game played at the highest available stakes at a particular venue. Also, a description of the quality of a player's performance when he or she is playing at the top of his or her ability.

action   A fold, check, call, bet, or raise. For certain situations, doing something formally connected with the game that conveys information about your hand might also be considered as having taken action. Examples would be showing your cards at the end of the hand or indicating the number of cards you are taking at draw.

aggressive action   A wager that could enable a player to win a pot without a showdown; a bet or raise.

all-in   When you have put all of your playable money and chips into the pot during the course of a hand, you are said to be *all-in*.

ante   A prescribed amount posted by all players before the start of a hand. (See photo 1.)

backdoor   Making a hand other than the one intended.

bad beat   A hand that is beaten by a lucky draw.

bet   The act of placing a wager in turn into the pot on any betting round. Also the chips put into the pot.

big blind (BB)   The largest blind in a game.

big slick   In Hold'em, a hand that contains an ace and a king (A-K). (See photo 2.)

blind   A required bet made before any cards are dealt.

blind game   A game that utilizes a blind.

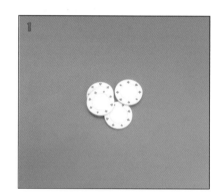

board The board on which a waiting list is kept for players wanting seats in specific games. Also, cards face up on the table common to each of the hands.

board card A community card in the center of the table, as in Hold'em or Omaha. (See photo 3.)

boxed card A card that appears face up in the deck when all other cards are face down.

bring-in In Seven-Card Stud, the forced bet on the first round of betting made by the player with the lowest card showing.

broken game A game no longer in action.

burn card After the initial round of cards is dealt, the first card off the deck in each round that is placed under a chip in the pot, for security purposes. To do so is to *burn the card;* the card itself is called the *burn card.* (See photo 4.)

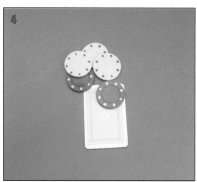

busted hand A worthless hand. Also, a hand that fails to complete a flush or straight.

button A player who is in the designated dealer position. See *dealer button.*

button games Games in which a dealer button is used.

buy-in The minimum amount of money required to enter any game.

capped Describes the situation in limit poker in which the maximum number of raises on the betting round has been reached.

cards speak The face value of a hand in a showdown is the true value of the hand, regardless of a verbal announcement.

chase To play a hand that probably is second best or lower.

check To waive the right to initiate the betting in a round, but to retain the right to act if another player initiates the betting.

check-raise   To waive the right to bet (check) until a bet has been made by an opponent, and then to increase the bet (raise) by at least an equal amount when it is your turn to act.

collection   The fee charged in a game (taken either out of the pot or from each player). Also known as the *rake*.

collection drop   A fee charged for each hand dealt.

color change   A request to change the chips from one denomination to another.

common card   A card dealt face up to be used by all players at the showdown in Stud Poker in which there are insufficient cards left in the deck to deal each player a card individually. (See photo 5.)

community cards   The cards dealt face up in the center of the table that can be used by all players to form their best hand in the games of Hold'em and Omaha. (See photo 6.)

complete the bet   To increase an all-in bet or forced bet to a full bet in limit poker.

connectors   Two sequential cards, such as A–K or 4–5. (See photo 7.)

cut   To divide the deck into two sections in such a manner as to change the order of the cards. (See photo 8.)

cut-card   Another term for the bottom card.

dead card   A card that is not legally playable.

dead collection blind   A fee posted by the player who has the dealer button, used in some games as an alternative method of seat rental or rake.

dead hand   A hand that is not legally playable.

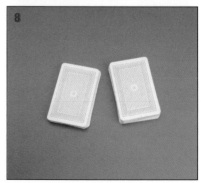

dead man's hand   Two pair, black aces and black eights, plus a fifth card. According to a legend, Wild Bill Hickok was shot during a poker game in Deadwood, South Dakota, holding this hand. (See photo 9.)

dead money   Chips that are taken into the center of the pot because they are not considered part of a particular player's bet.

deal   To give each player cards, or to put cards on the board. In many card games, each deal refers to the entire process, from the shuffling and dealing of cards until the pot is awarded to the winner.

deal off   To take all the blinds and the button before changing seats or leaving the table. That is, participate through all the blind positions and the dealer position.

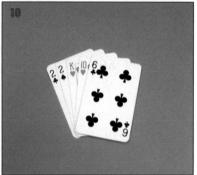

deal twice   When there is no more betting, agreeing to have the rest of the cards to come determine only half the pot, removing those cards, and dealing again for the other half of the pot.

dealer button   A flat disk that indicates the player who is in the dealing position for that hand (if there is not a house dealer). Usually referred to as *the button.*

deck   A set of playing-cards. In these games, the deck consists of either 52 cards in Seven-Card Stud, Hold'em, and Omaha; or 53 cards (including the Joker), often used in Ace-to-Five Lowball and Draw High.

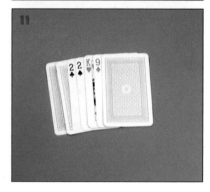

deuce(s)   One or more twos. (See photo 10 for a pair of deuces.)

discard(s)   In a draw game, to throw cards out of your hand to make room for replacements, or the card(s) thrown away; the *muck.*

down cards   Cards that are dealt face down in a Stud game. (See photo 11.)

draw   The poker form in which players are given the opportunity to replace cards in the hand. Also, the act of replacing cards in the hand. Alternatively, the point in the deal where replacing is done is called *the draw.*

draw to a flush/straight   Holding four cards of a flush or straight and anticipating being dealt a card that will complete it. (See photo 12 for a draw to a flush.)

face card   A king, queen, or jack. (See photo 13.)

fixed limit   In limit poker, any betting structure in which the amount of the bet on each particular round is pre-set.

flashed card   A card that is partially exposed.

floorperson   A casino employee who seats players and makes decisions.

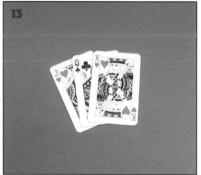

flop   In Hold'em or Omaha, the three community cards that are turned simultaneously after the first round of betting is complete. (See photo 14.)

flush   A poker hand consisting of five cards of the same suit. (See photo 15.)

fold   To throw away a hand and relinquish all interest in a pot.

fouled hand   A dead hand.

fourth street   The second up card in Seven-Card Stud or the first board card after the flop in Hold'em (also called the *turn card*).

forced bet   A required wager to start the action on the first betting round (the normal way action begins in a Stud game).

freeroll   A chance to win something at no risk or cost.

full buy   A buy-in of at least the minimum requirement of chips needed for a particular game.

full house   A hand consisting of three-of-a-kind and a pair. (See photo 16.)

hand   All of a player's personal cards. Also, the five cards determining the poker ranking. Also, a single poker deal.

heads-up play   Only two players involved in play.

hole cards   The cards dealt face down to a player. (See photo 17.)

inside straight   Four cards of a straight missing an inside card: 3-4-6-7, for example. A player who then is dealt a five "makes" the inside straight. (See photo 18.)

Joker   The Joker is a "partially wild card" in High Draw Poker and Ace-to-Five Lowball. In High Draw, it is used for aces, straights, and flushes. In Lowball, the Joker is the lowest unmatched rank in a hand. (See photo 19.)

kicker   The highest unpaired card that helps determine the value of a five-card poker hand. (See photo 20 for a hand with a kicker.)

kill (or kill blind)   An oversize blind, usually twice the size of the big blind and doubling the limit. Sometimes a *half-kill,* which increases the blind and limits by 50 percent, is used. A kill can be either voluntary or mandatory. The most common requirements of a mandatory kill are for winning two pots in a row at Lowball and other games, or for *scooping* (winning all of) a pot in High-Low Split.

kill button   A button used in a lowball game to indicate a player who has won two pots in a row and is required to kill the pot.

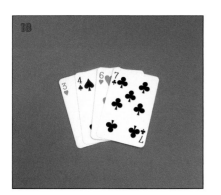

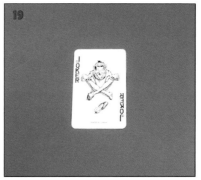

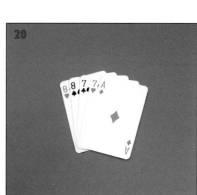

kill pot   A pot with a forced kill by the winner of the two previous pots, or the winner of an entire pot of sufficient size in a High-Low Split game.

leg up   Being in a situation equivalent to having won the previous pot, and thus liable to have to kill the following pot if you win the current pot.

list   The ordered roster of players waiting for a game.

live blind   A blind bet that gives a player the option of raising if no one else has raised.

lock-up   A chip marker that holds a seat for a player.

Lowball   A draw game in which the lowest hand wins.

low card   The lowest up card in Seven-Card Stud, which is required to make the initial fixed or minimum bet.

miscall   An incorrect verbal declaration of the ranking of a hand.

misdeal   A mistake in the dealing of a hand that causes the cards to be reshuffled and a new hand to be dealt.

missed blind   A required bet that is not posted when it is your turn to do so.

muck   The pile of discards gathered face down in the center of the table by the dealer. Also, to discard a hand. (See photo 21.)

no-limit   A betting structure in which players are allowed to wager any or all of their chips in one bet.

opener   The player who made the first voluntary bet.

opener button   A button used to indicate who opened a particular pot in a draw game.

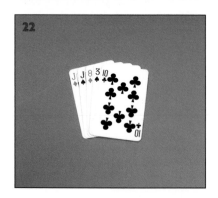

openers   In Jacks-or-Better Draw, the cards held by the player who opens the pot that show the hand qualifies to be opened. (See photo 22.)

option   The choice to raise a bet given to a player with a blind.

overblind   Also called *oversize blind.* A blind used in some pots that is bigger than the regular big blind, and which usually increases the stakes proportionally.

overcard   Card on the board that is higher than the pair you have.

pass   To decline to bet. Also, to decline to call a wager, at which point you must discard your hand and have no further interest in the pot.

pat   Not drawing any cards in a draw game.

play behind   To have chips in play that are not in front of you (allowed only when waiting for chips that are already purchased). This differs from table stakes.

play the board   Using all five community cards for your hand in Hold'em.

play over   To play in a seat when the occupant is absent.

playover box   A clear plastic box used to cover and protect the chips of an absent player when someone plays over that seat.

position   The relation of a player's seat to the blinds or the button. Also, the order of acting on a betting round or deal. (See photo 23.)

pot-limit   The betting structure of a game in which you are allowed to bet up to the amount of the pot.

potting out   Agreeing with another player to take money out of a pot, often to buy food, cigarettes, or drinks, or to make side bets.

protected hand   A hand of cards that the player is physically holding or has topped with a chip or some other object to prevent a fouled hand.

push   When a new dealer replaces an existing dealer at a particular table.

pushing bets   The situation in which two or more players make an agreement to return bets to each other when one of them wins a pot in which the other or others play. Also called *saving bets.*

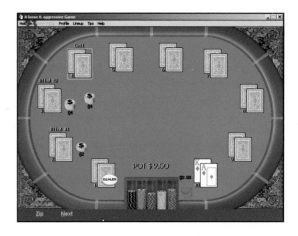

rack A container in which chips are stored while being transported. Also, a tray in front of the dealer, used to hold chips and cards. (See photo 24.)

raise To increase the amount of a previous wager. This increase must meet certain specifications, depending on the game, to reopen the betting and count toward a limit on the number of raises allowed.

reraise To raise someone's raise.

ring game Poker game where players can leave at any time or join if there is an open seat. Also called a *side game*.

saving bets Same as *pushing bets*.

scoop To win both the high and low portions of a pot in a split-pot game. (See photo 25.)

scramble A face-down mixing of the cards.

setup Two suited decks, each with different-colored backs, to replace the current decks in a game.

side pot A separate pot sometimes formed when one or more players are all-in.

short buy A buy-in that is less than the required minimum buy-in.

showdown The final act of determining the winner of the pot after all betting has been completed by comparing hands. (See photo 26, which shows a pair of tens beating a pair of eights.)

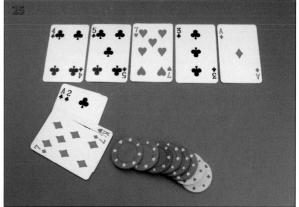

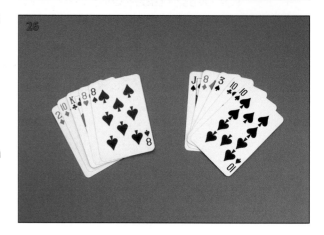

shuffle The act of mixing the cards before a hand. (See photo 27.)

small blind (SB) In a game with multiple blind bets, the smallest blind.

split pot A pot that is divided among players, either because of a tie for the best hand or by agreement prior to the showdown.

splitting blinds When no one else has entered the pot, an agreement between the big blind and small blind to each take back their blind bets instead of playing the deal (*chopping*).

splitting openers In High Draw Jacks-or-Better Poker, dividing openers in hopes of making a different type of hand. Example: You open the pot with a pair of aces. One of your aces is a spade, as are the three other cards in the hand. If you throw away the non-spade ace to go for the flush, you announce to the table, "Splitting openers."

stack Chips in front of a player. (See photo 28.)

straddle An additional blind bet placed after the forced blinds, usually double the big blind in size; or in Lowball, a multiple-blind game.

straight Five cards in consecutive rank. (See photo 29.)

straight flush Five cards in consecutive rank of the same suit. (See photo 30.)

street Cards dealt on a particular round in stud games. For instance, the fourth card in a player's hand is often known as *fourth street,* the sixth card as *sixth street,* and so on.

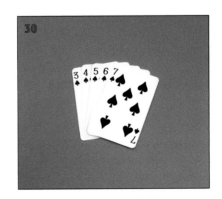

string raise   A bet made in more than one motion, without the declaration of a raise (not allowed).

stub   The portion of the deck that has not been dealt.

suited connectors   Two sequential cards that are of the same suit, such as A♦-K♦ or 4♥-5♥. (See photo 31.)

supervisor   A card-room employee qualified to make rulings, such as a floorperson, shift supervisor, or the card-room manager.

table stakes   The amount of money you have on the table. This is the maximum amount that you can lose or that anyone can win from you on any one hand. Also, the requirement that players can wager only the money in front of them at the start of a hand, and can buy more chips only between hands.

tells   A player's action(s) that may indicate the strength of the hand the player holds.

time   An expression used to stop the action on a hand; equivalent to *hold it.*

time collection   A time-based fee for a seat rental, paid in advance.

tournament   A poker competition, normally with an entry fee and prizes.

treys   A pair of threes. (See photo 32.)

trips   Three-of-a-kind. (See photo 33.)

turn card   The fourth-street card in Hold'em or Omaha. (See photo 34.)

up cards   Cards that are dealt face up for opponents to see in stud games.

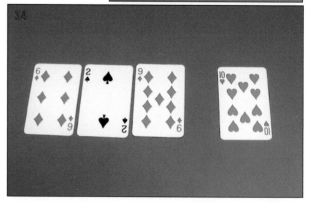

wager   To bet or raise. Also, the chips used for betting or raising.

zombie   A player who shows no emotions, no *tells,* that allow other players to guess the player's hand.

Index

W

Western movies, draw poker, 30
Whiskey (Whisky), draw poker variation, 60
widow, Whiskey (Whisky), 60
wild cards, 56, 92, 95, 170, 175
Wild Widow, Spit in the Ocean variation, 61
Wilson Software, Turbo Texas Hold'em, 202
winners, etiquette rules, 25
winnings, tax issues, 29
Woolworth, stud poker variation, 93

World Poker Tour (WPT), 243, 244, 247, 248
World Series of Poker (WSoP), 240, 243, 244, 246, 248

Y

Yahoo.com, free-poker site, 197

Z

zero (check) bet, 21, 41, 90, 102

Teach Yourself VISUALLY™ books...

Whether you want to knit, sew, or crochet...strum a guitar or play the piano...train a dog or create a scrapbook...make the most of Windows XP or touch up your Photoshop CS2 skills, Teach Yourself VISUALLY books get you into action instead of bogging you down in lengthy instructions. All Teach Yourself VISUALLY books are written by experts on the subject and feature:

- Hundreds of color photos or screenshots that demonstrate each step or skill

- Step-by-step instructions accompanying each photo
- FAQs that answer common questions and suggest solutions to common problems
- Information about each skill clearly presented on a two- or four-page spread so you can learn by seeing and doing
- A design that makes it easy to review a particular topic

Look for Teach Yourself VISUALLY books to help you learn a variety of skills—all with the proven visual learning approaches you enjoyed in this book.

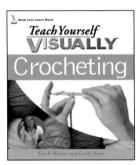

0-7645-9641-1

Teach Yourself VISUALLY™ Crocheting

Picture yourself crocheting accessories, garments, and great home décor items. It's a relaxing hobby, and this is the relaxing way to learn! This Visual guide *shows* you the basics, beginning with the tools and materials needed and the basic stitches, then progresses through following patterns, creating motifs and fun shapes, and finishing details. A variety of patterns gets you started, and more advanced patterns get you hooked!

0-7645-9640-3

Teach Yourself VISUALLY™ Knitting

Get yourself some yarn and needles and get clicking! This Visual guide *shows* you the basics of knitting—photo by photo and stitch by stitch. You begin with the basic knit and purl patterns and advance to bobbles, knots, cables, openwork, and finishing techniques—knitting as you go. With fun, innovative patterns from top designer Sharon Turner, you'll be creating masterpieces in no time!

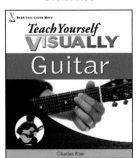

0-7645-9642-X

Teach Yourself VISUALLY™ Guitar

Pick up this book and a guitar and start strumming! *Teach Yourself VISUALLY Guitar* shows you the basics photo by photo and note by note. You begin with essential chords and techniques and progress through suspensions, bass runs, hammer-ons, and barre chords. As you learn to read chord charts, tablature, and lead sheets, you can play any number of songs, from rock to folk to country. The chord chart and scale appendices are ready references for use long after you master the basics.

designed for visual learners like you!

0-7645-7927-4

Teach Yourself VISUALLY™ Windows® XP, 2nd Edition

Clear step-by-step screenshots *show* you how to tackle more than 150 Windows XP tasks. Learn how to draw, fill, and edit shapes, set up and secure an Internet account, load images from a digital camera, copy tracks from music CDs, defragment your hard drive, and more.

0-7645-8840-0

Teach Yourself VISUALLY™ Photoshop® CS2

Clear step-by-step screenshots *show* you how to tackle more than 150 Photoshop CS2 tasks. Learn how to import images from digital cameras, repair damaged photos, browse and sort images in Bridge, change image size and resolution, paint and draw with color, create duotone images, apply layer and filter effects, and more.